FREE IMAGININGS

BY, ACE SPRINGER

CONTENTS OF THIS BOOK:
THIS BOOK CONTAINS IMAGES OF WHAT I CALL "AUTOMATIC DRAWING"

WHICH IS A CONCEPT I THINK I FIRST HEARD ABOUT IN A COLLEGE
PSYCHOLOGY CLASS IN REFERENCE TO "AUTOMATIC WRITING" IN
WHICH THE CONSCIOUS THINKING BRAIN IS SUPPOSED TO BE
SOMEWHAT DEACTIVATED WHILE THE SUBCONSCIOUS LAYERS ARE ABLE
TO EMERGE BY THE USE OF YOUR NON- DOMINANT HAND TO WRITE
THINGS AND YOU ARE TO JUST WRITE WHATEVER COMES TO MIND.
CHOOSING THE INTENTION OF BEING NON-JUDGEMENTAL TOWARDS
WHAT COMES OUT WHILE IT IS COMING OUT. SO I HELD ONTO THIS
CONCEPT AND TRANSPOSED IT INTO MY CREATIVE WORLD AND
REALIZED THAT I DIDN'T MUCH ENJOY DRAWING CONCEPTS THAT I
CONSCIOUSLY KNEW OF ANYWAY…THE SUBCONSCIOUS AND
UNCONSCIOUS CHATTER OF LINEWORK WAS MUCH MORE AMUSING AND
GRATIFYING.

I BELIEVE THAT WE EACH CARRY SPECIFIC PREFERENCES FOR WHAT
WE ENJOY AESTHETICALLY AND IT IS MY PERSONAL BELIEF THAT
THESE EXIST TO HELP US
CONNECT WITH EACH OTHER (AND NOT TO DIVIDE US FROM ONE
ANOTHER).

SO I HOPE THAT SOME OF MY IMAGES CAN TOUCH THE PIECES OF YOU
THAT FEEL ONE THING OR ANOTHER AND I HOPE THAT YOU CAN CONNECT
WITH THOSE PIECES OF YOU THAT NEED TO FEEL THOSE THINGS.
I CHALLENGE YOU TO GAZE INTO THE MIRROR THAT IS YOUR/OUR
UNCONSCIOUS AND EXPLORE WHAT COMES UP…

I HOPE YOU ENJOY COLORING THESE PAGES!

SIDE NOTE FROM THE ARTIST:

I BELIEVE IN AND SEE MYSELF BEING A VERY
RAW PERSON AND
THEREFORE THESE DRAWINGS ARE ALL IN WHAT
I PERCEIVE AS THEIR MOST RAW FORMAT.

NO DIGITAL EDITING HAS OCCURED BEYOND
CROPPING, SIZING AND EQUALIZING THE
COLORS AMONGST THE PAGES (SOME OF THE
PAGES WERE ON NON-WHITE PAPER).

I HOPE YOU ENJOY THE "RAW FEEL"
OF THE SKETCHES.

THIS ADVENTURE CONTAINS THREE CHAPTERS:

-NATURAL
-EXTRATERRESTRIAL
-CEREBRAL

NATURAL

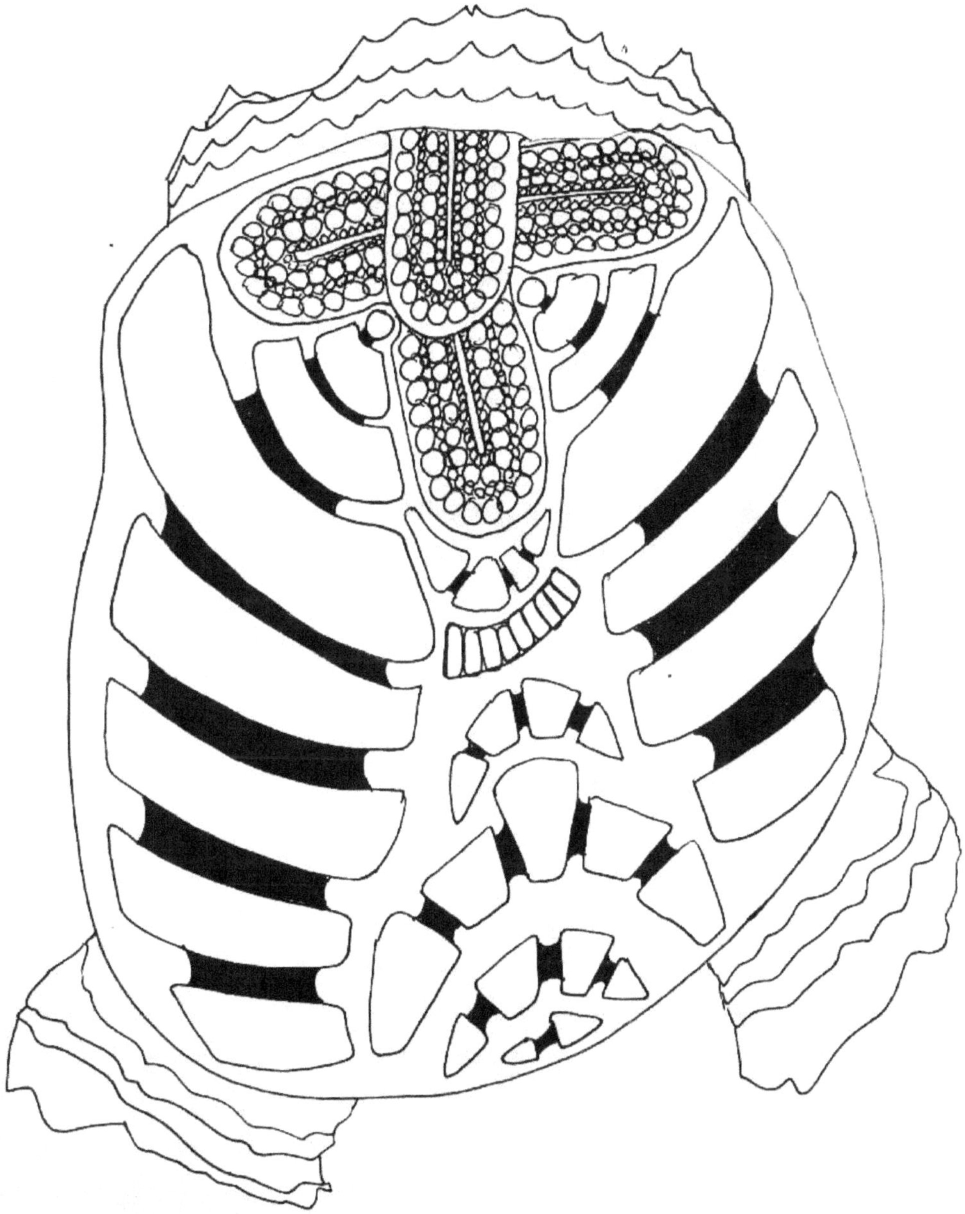

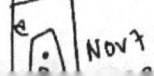

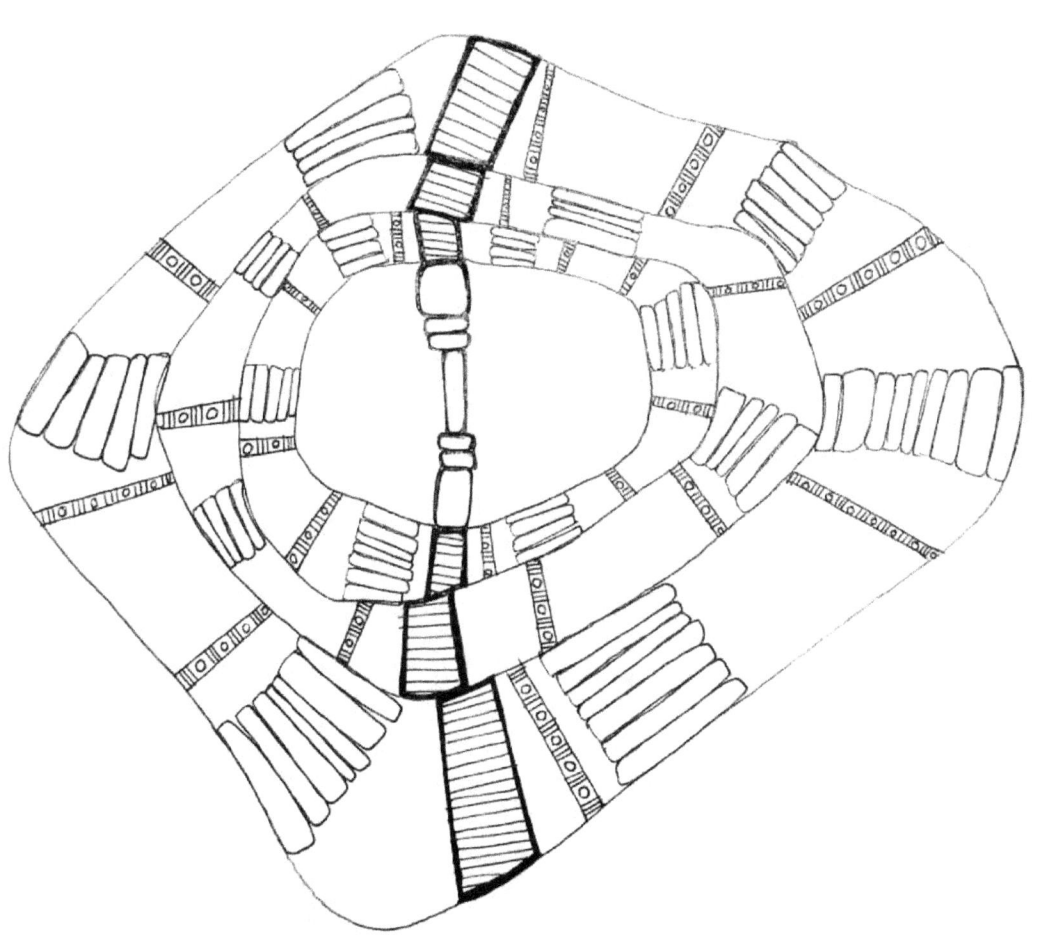

DEC14

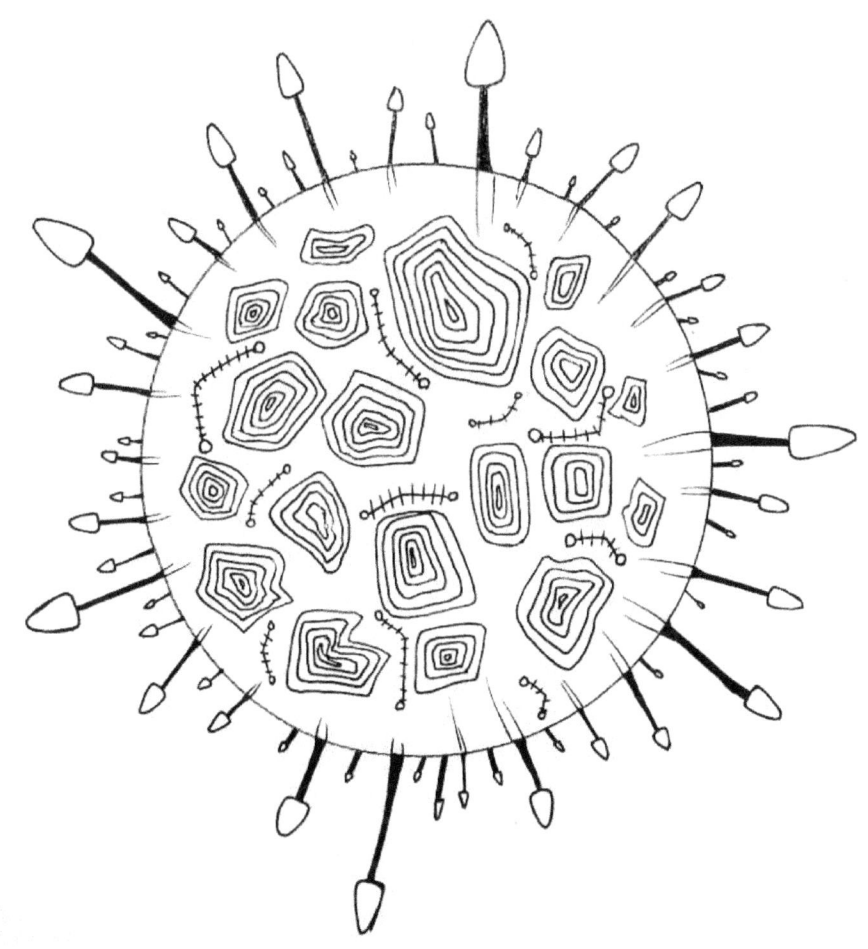

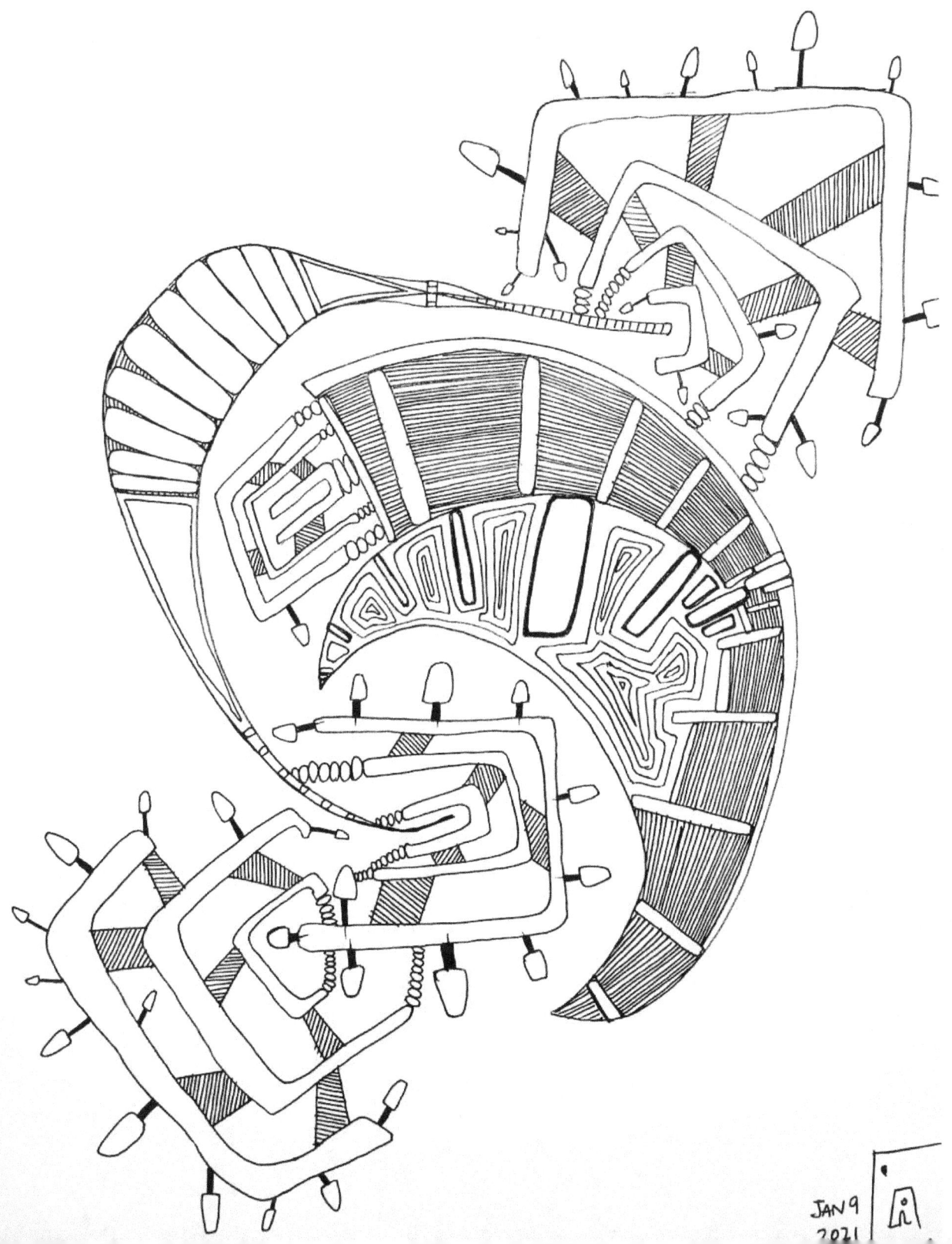

JAN 9
2021

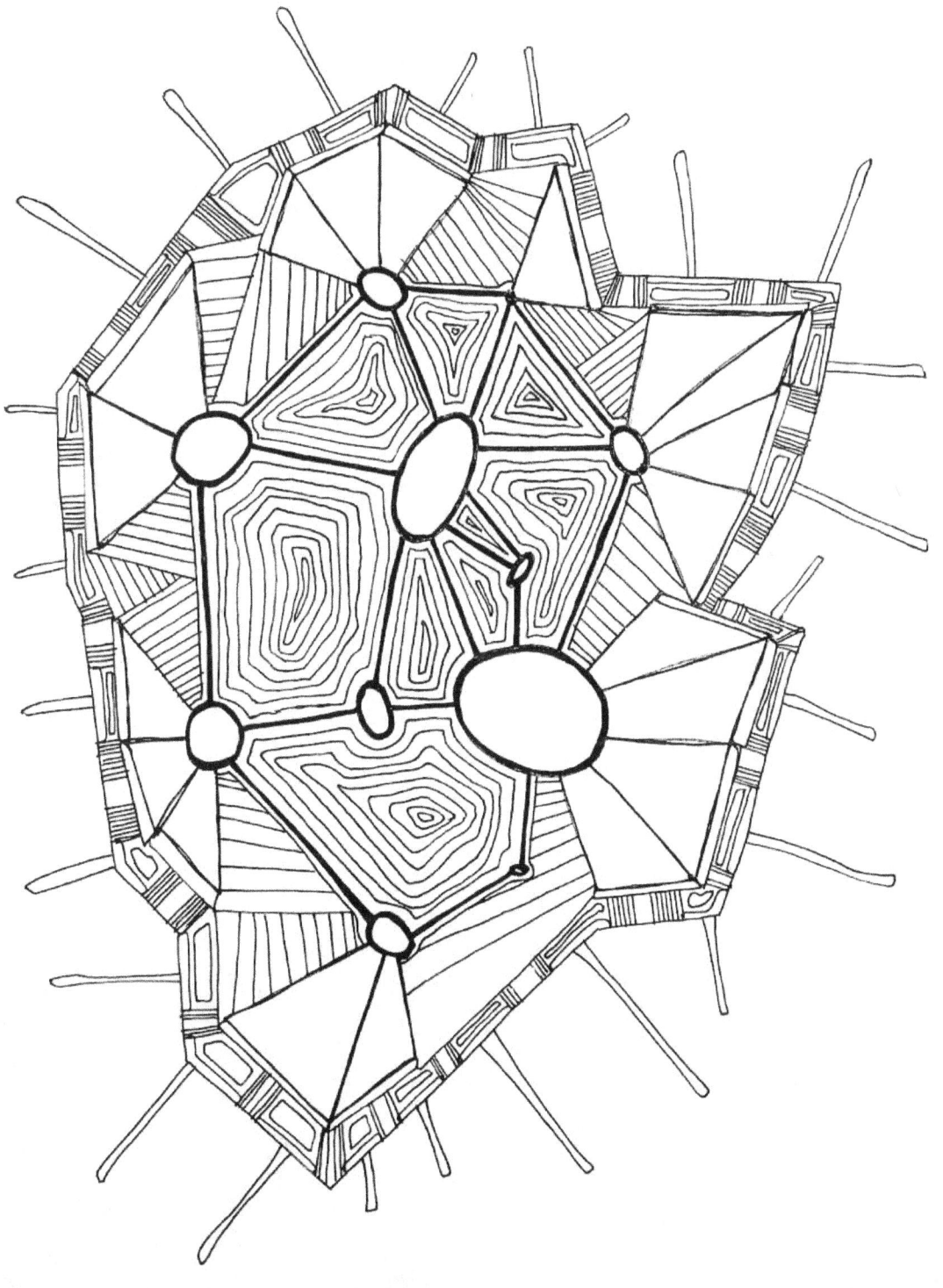

JAN 9
2021

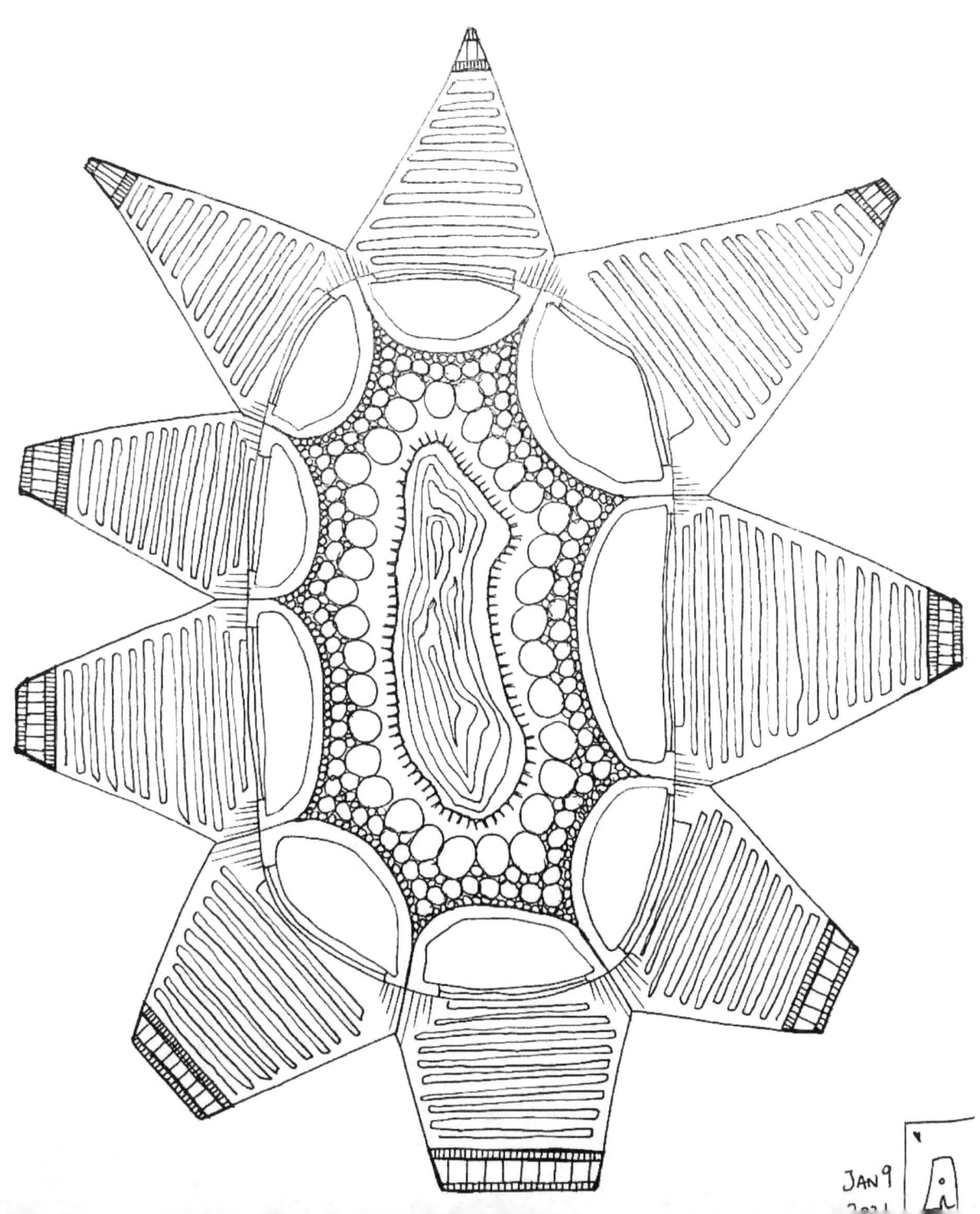

JAN 9

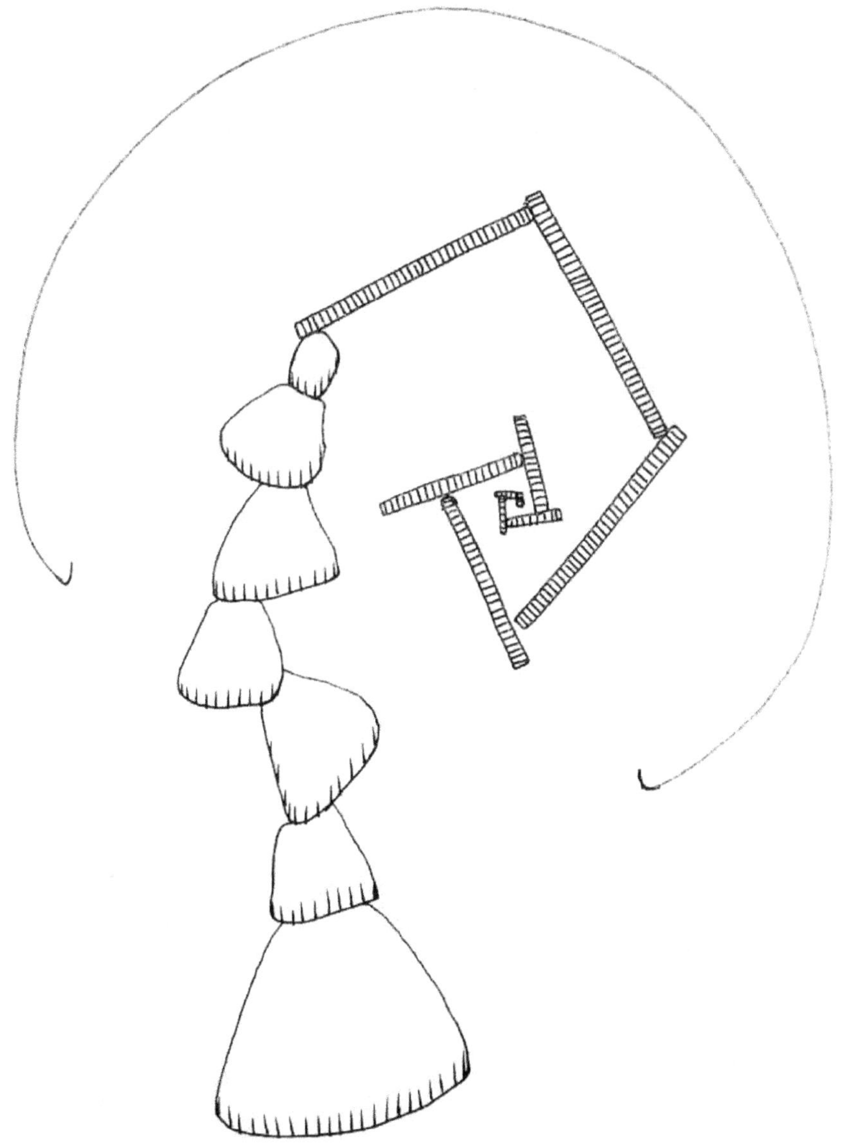

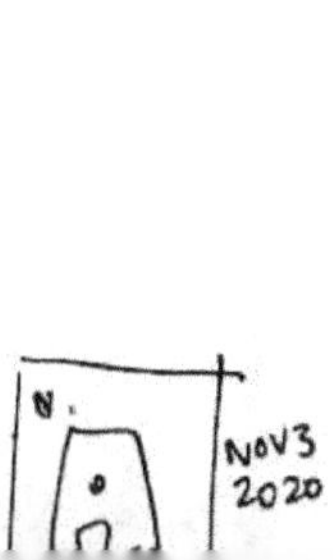

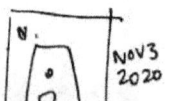

NOV3
2020

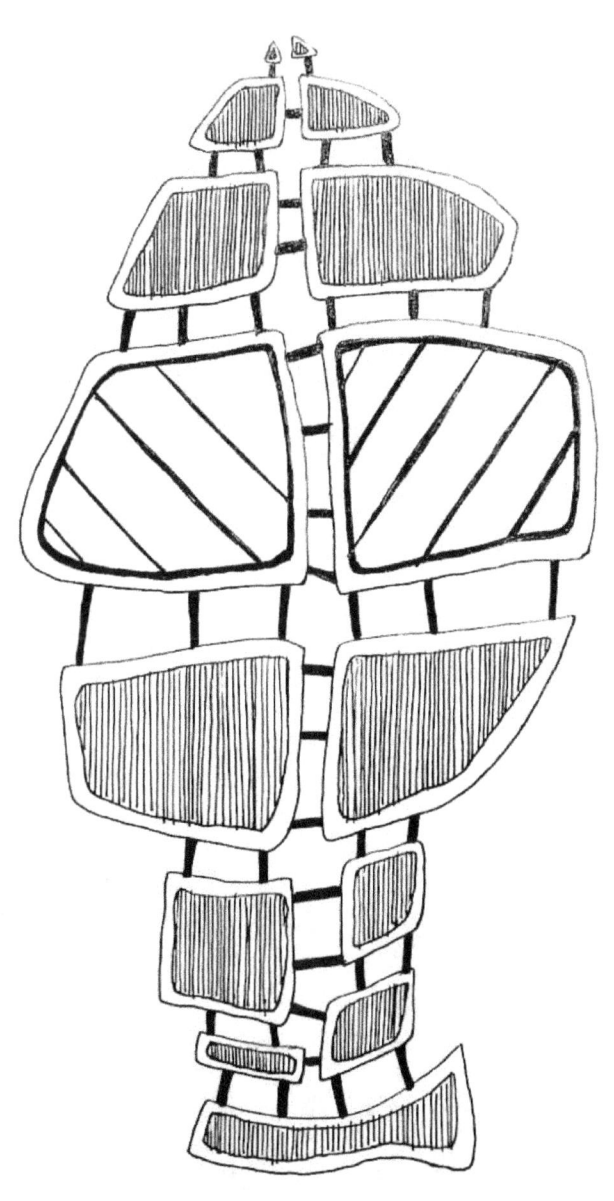

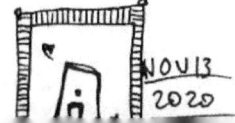

NOV 13
2020

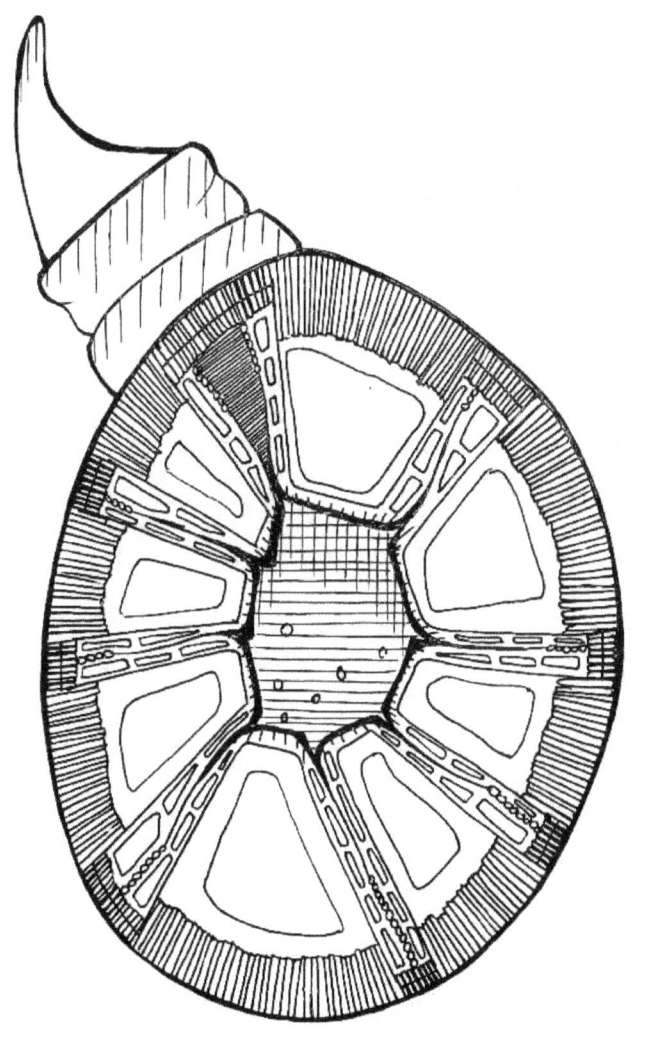

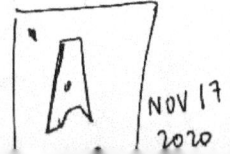
NOV 17
2020

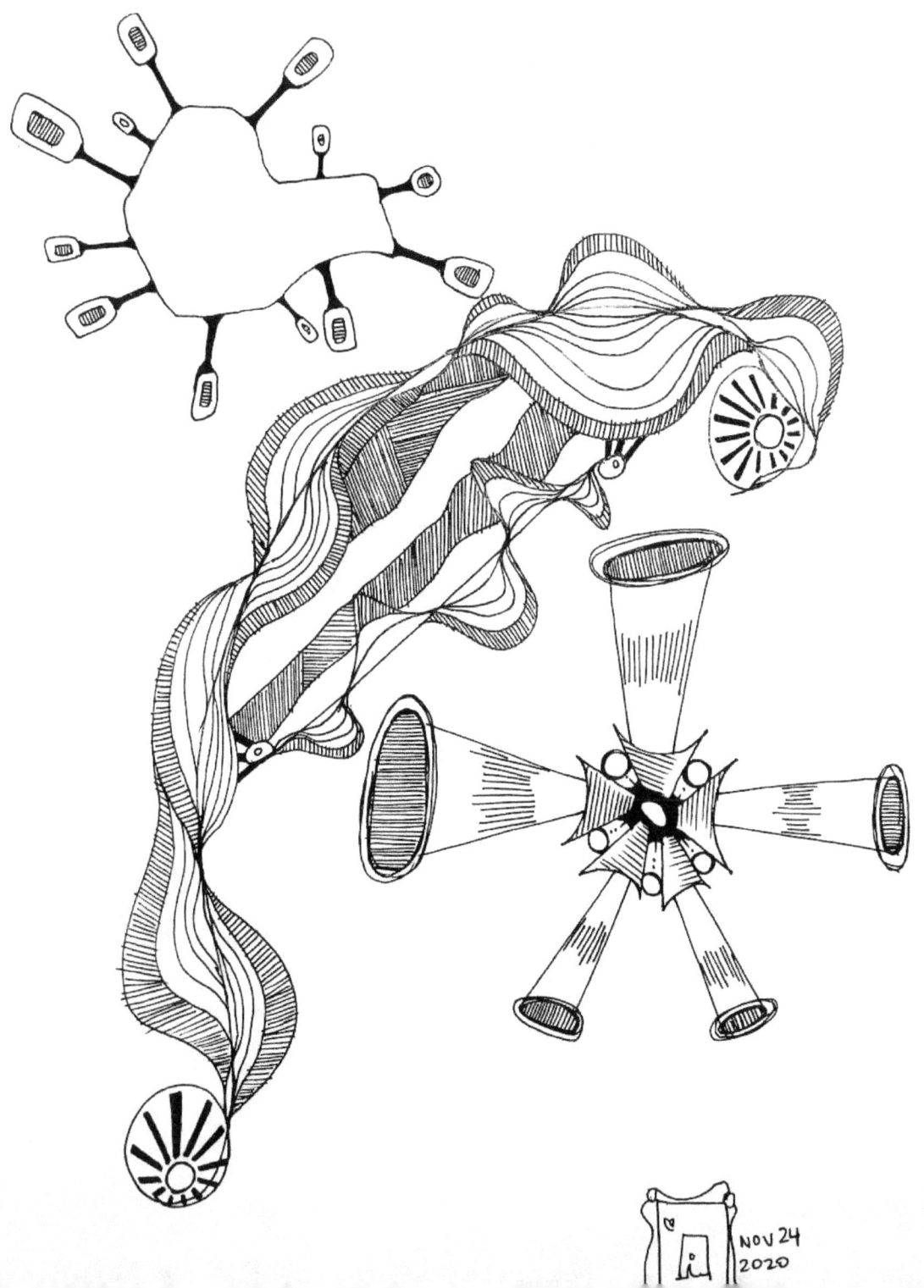

NOV 24
2020

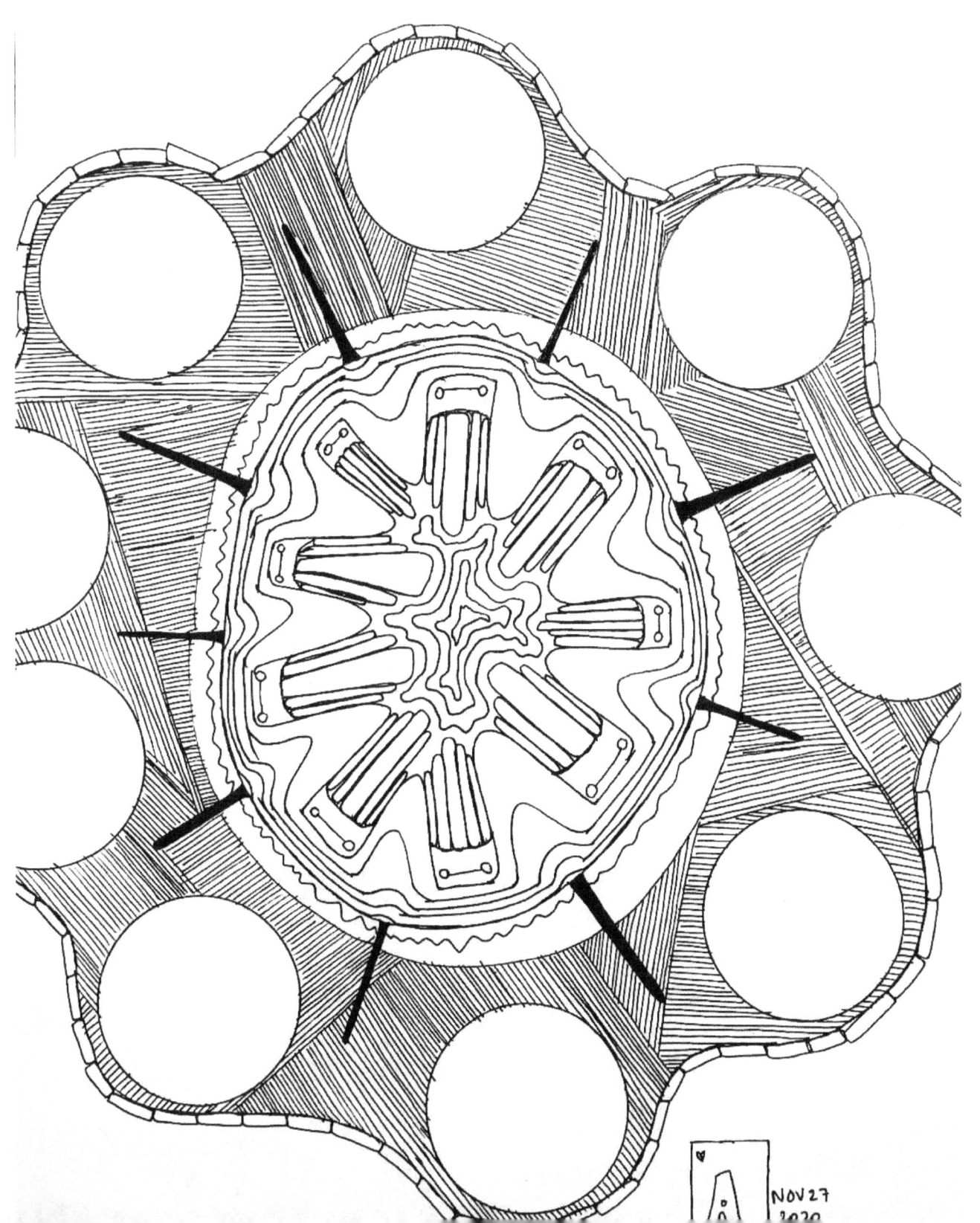

NOV 27
2020

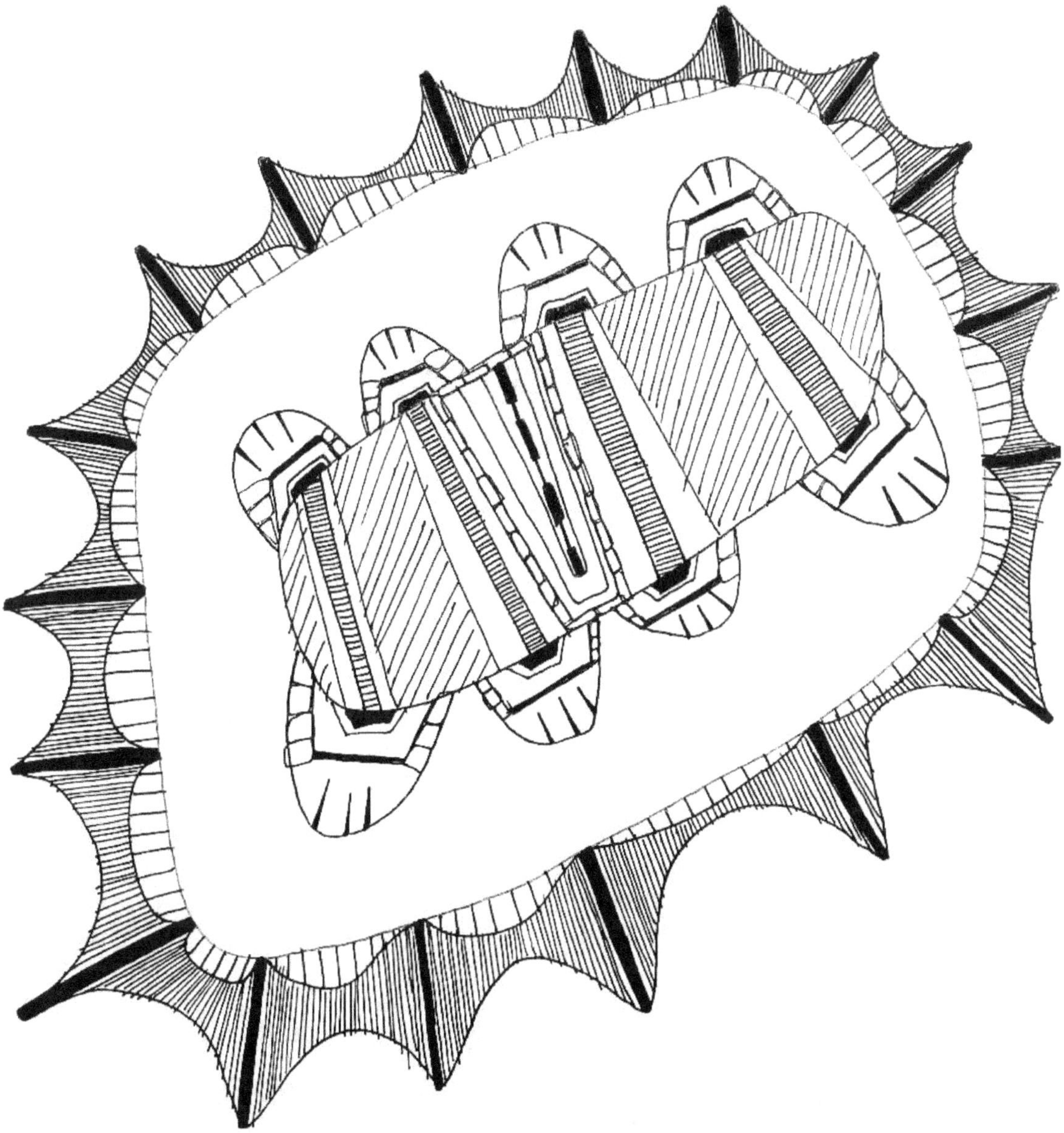

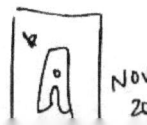

NOV 27
2020

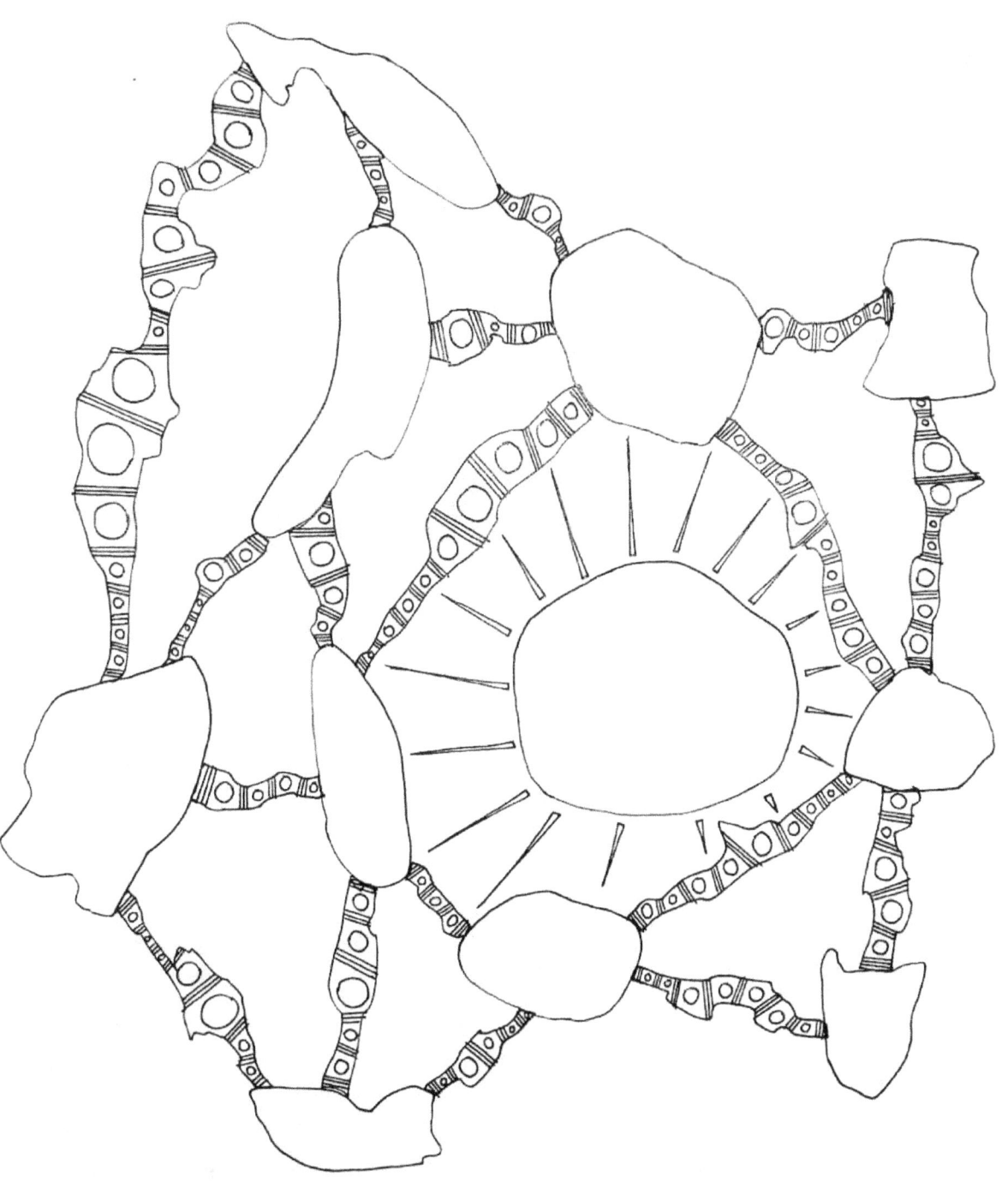

DEC14

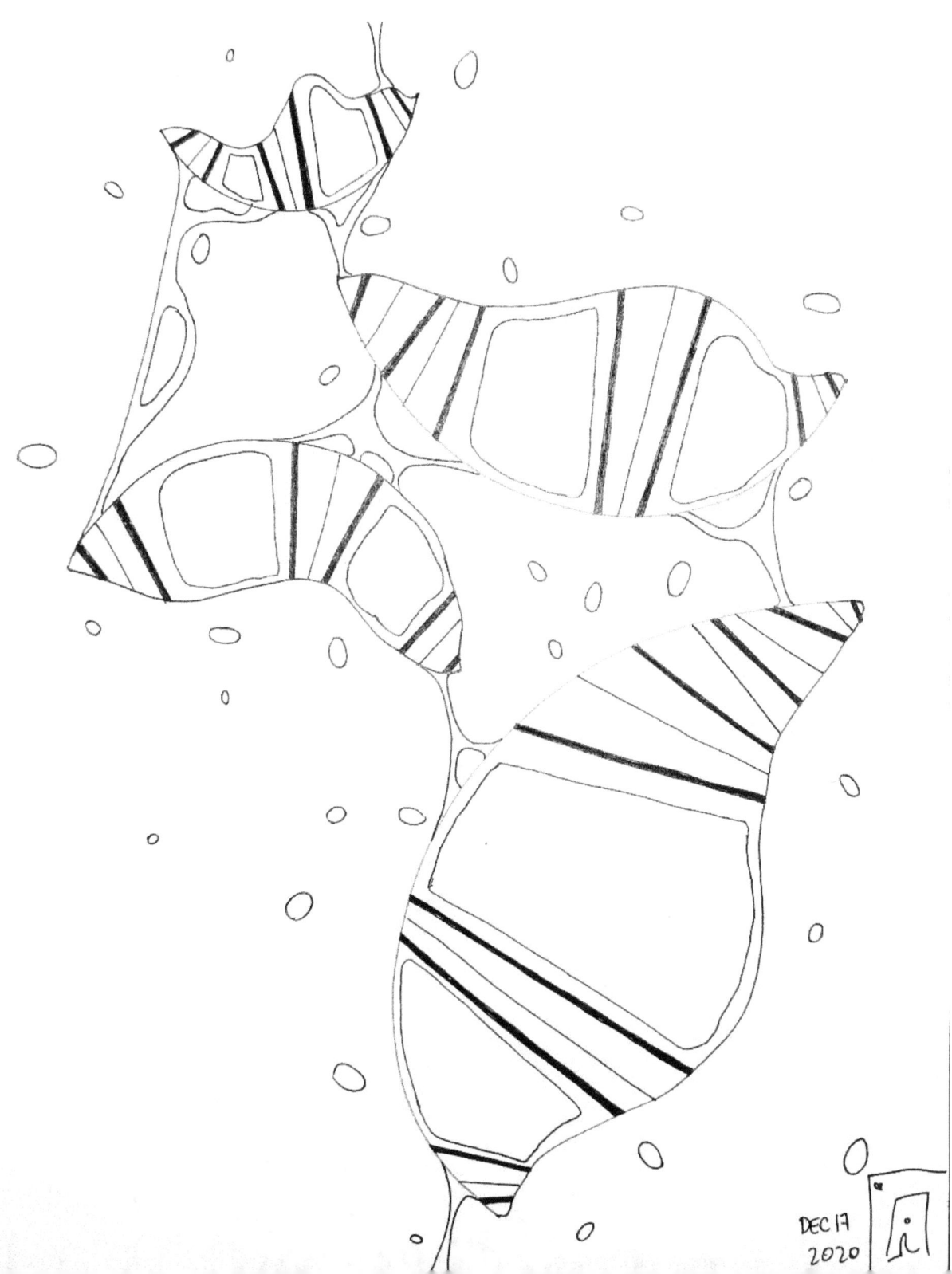

DEC 17
2020

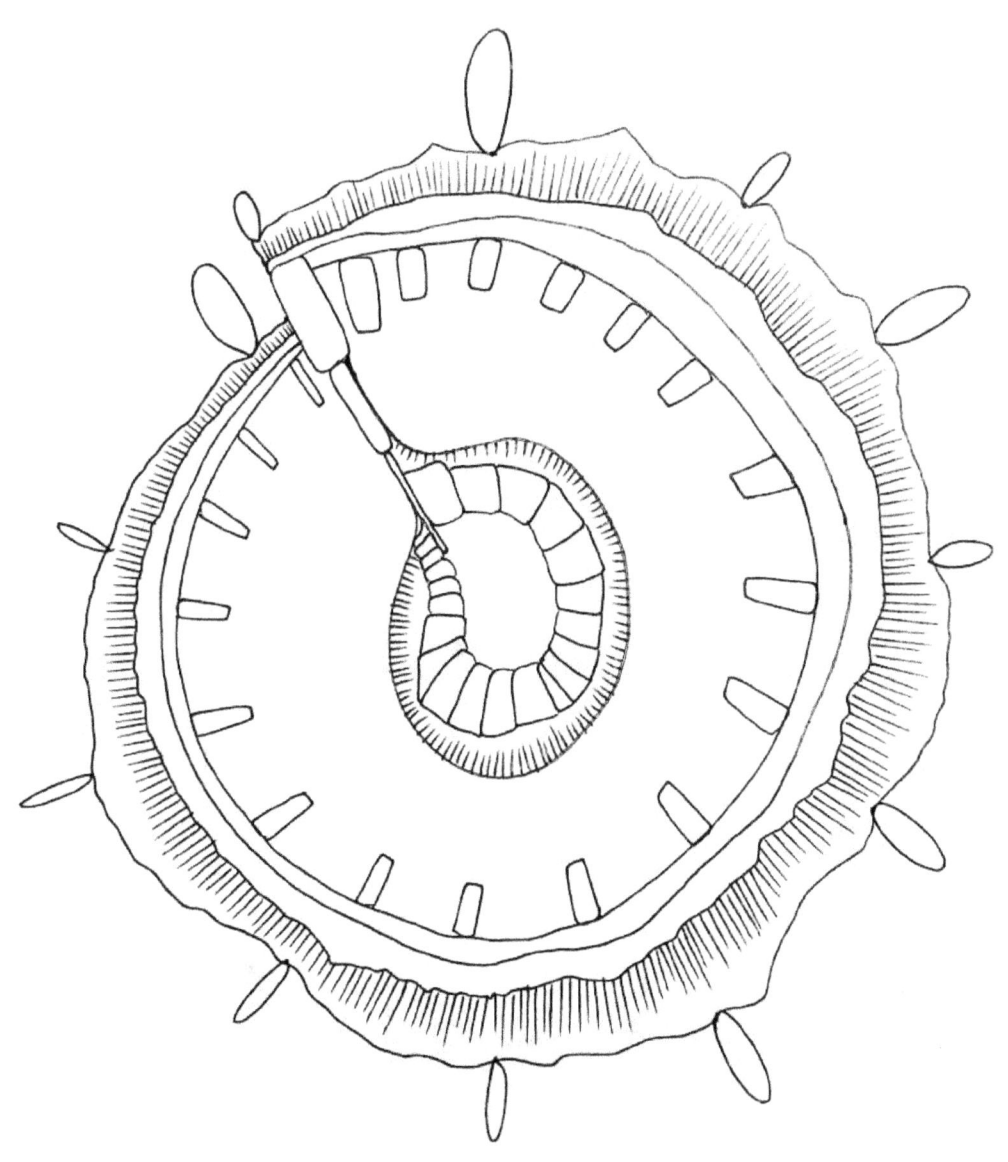

DEC 19

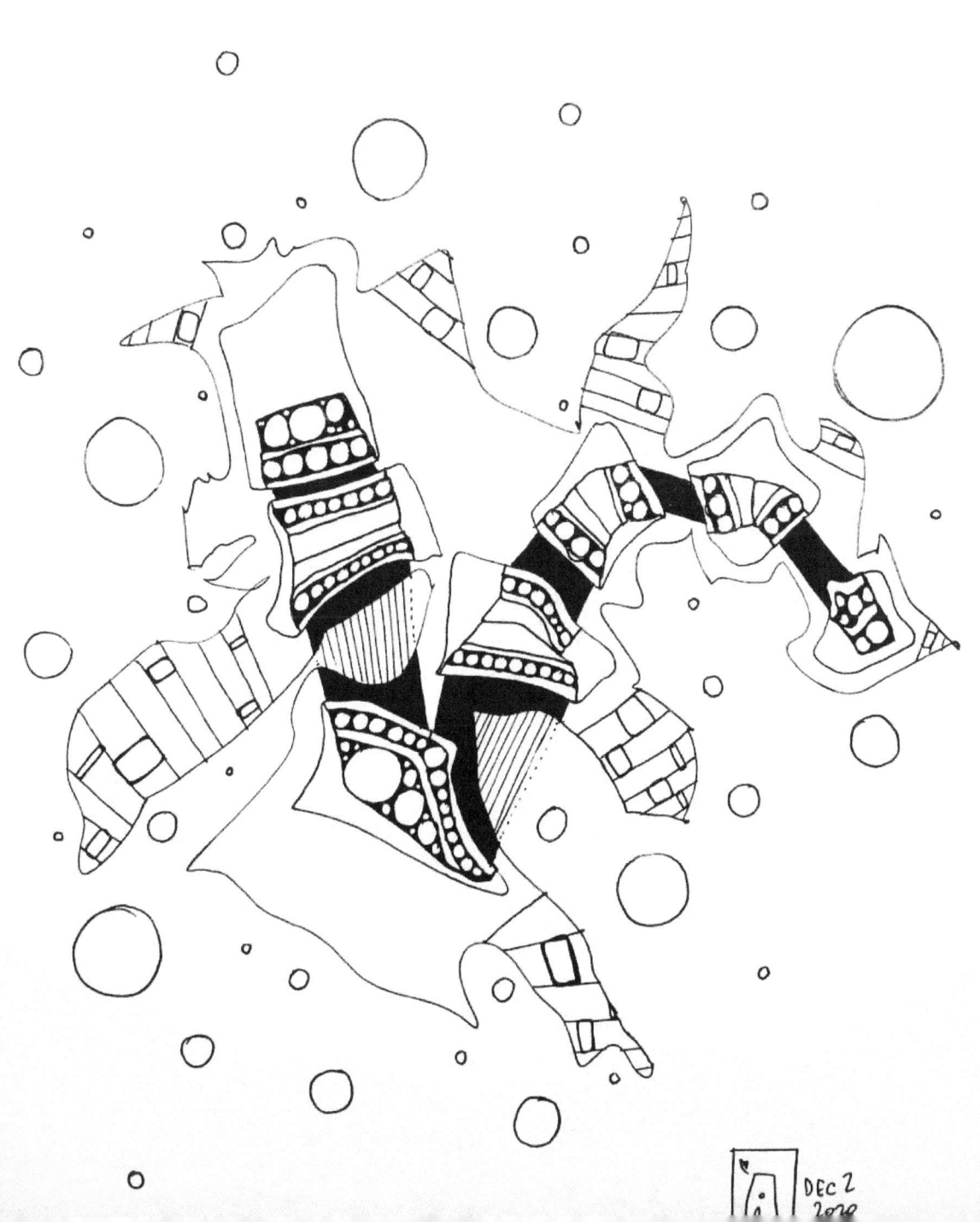

DEC 2
2020

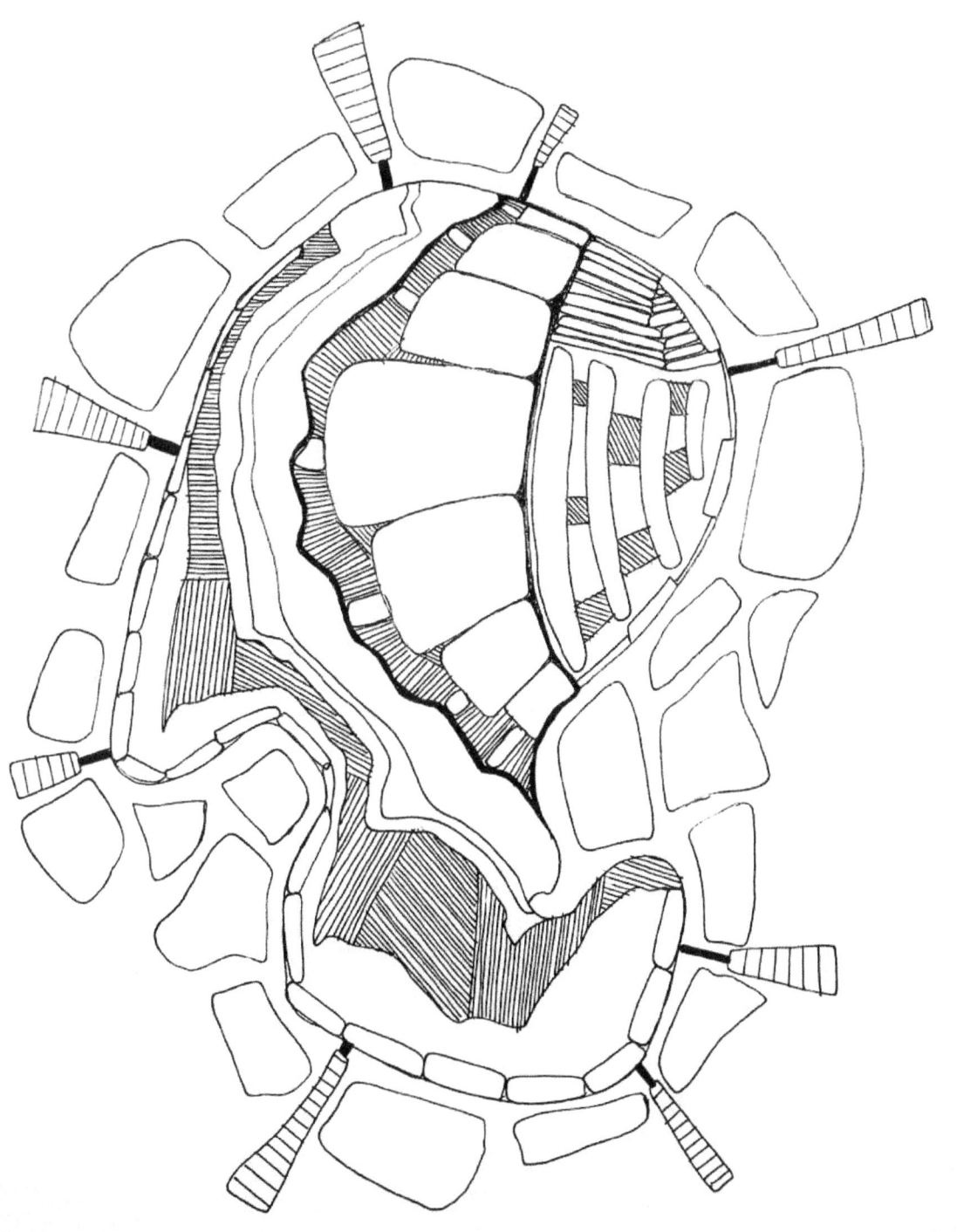

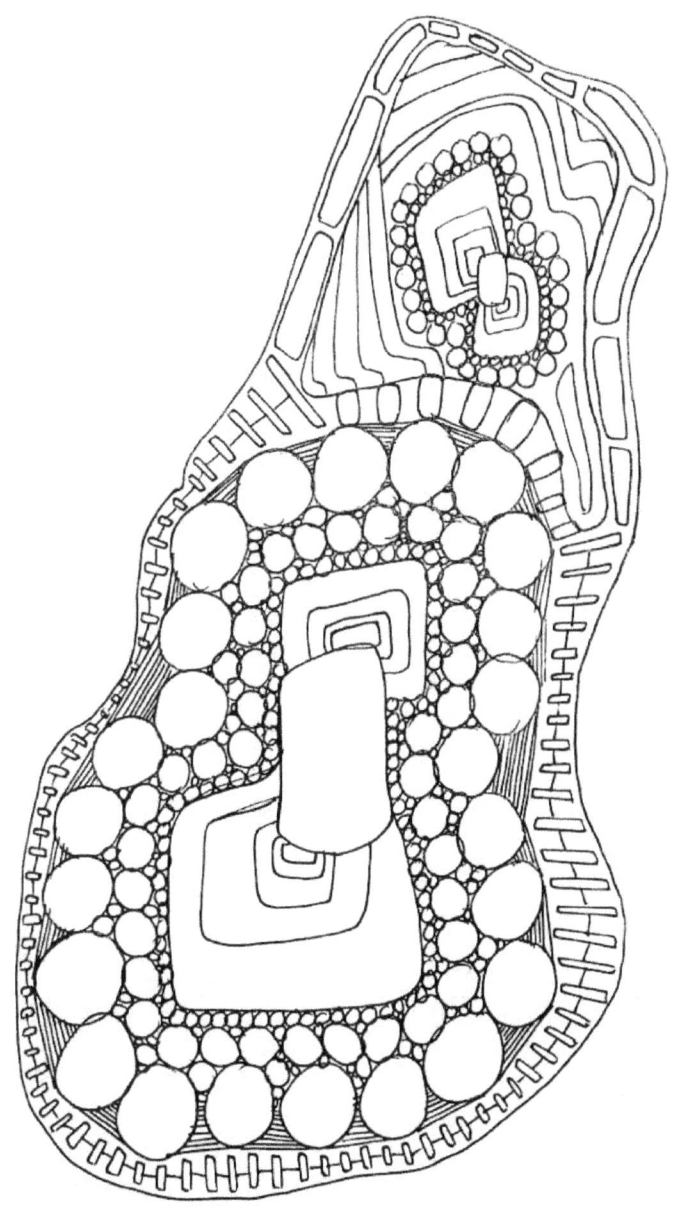

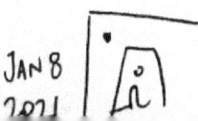

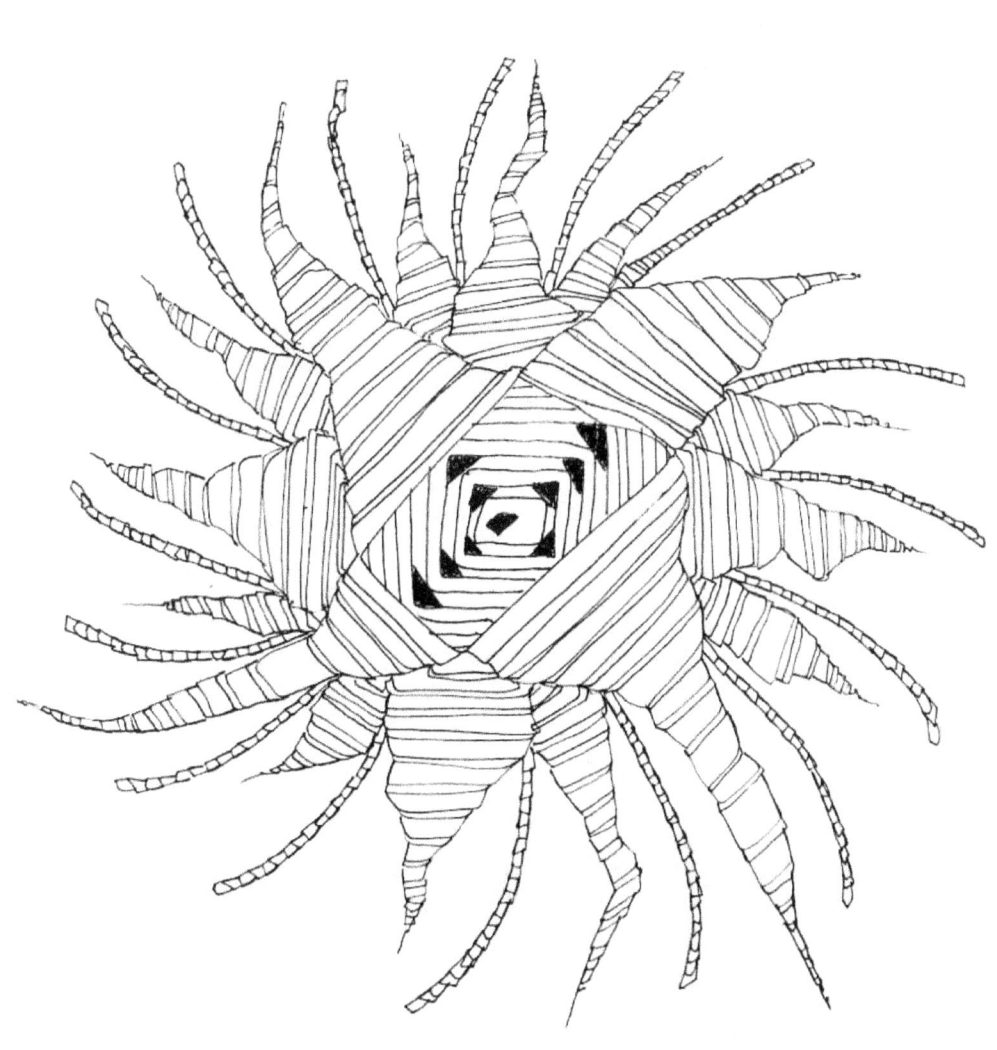

FFRIS-2019

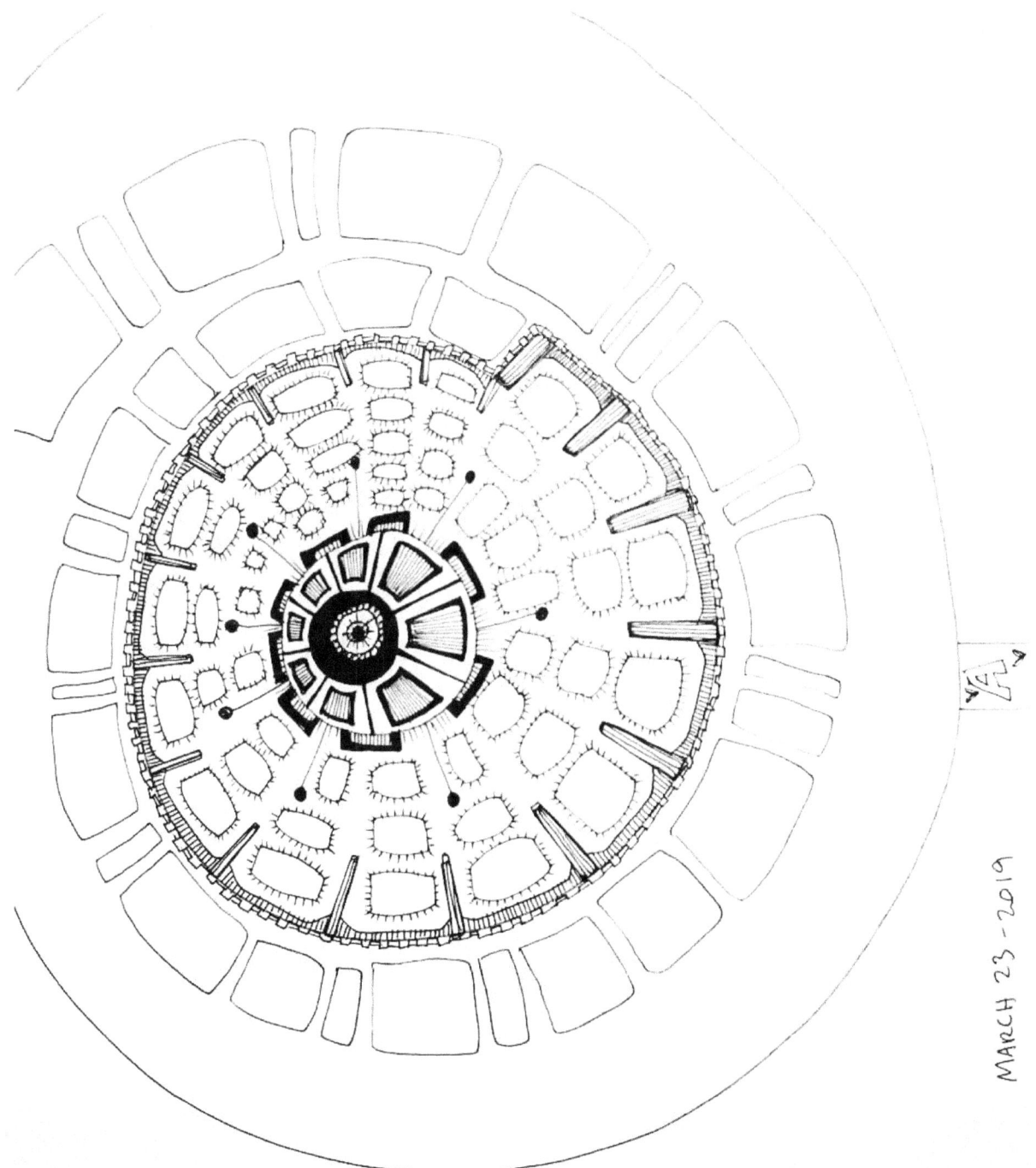

MARCH 23 - 2019

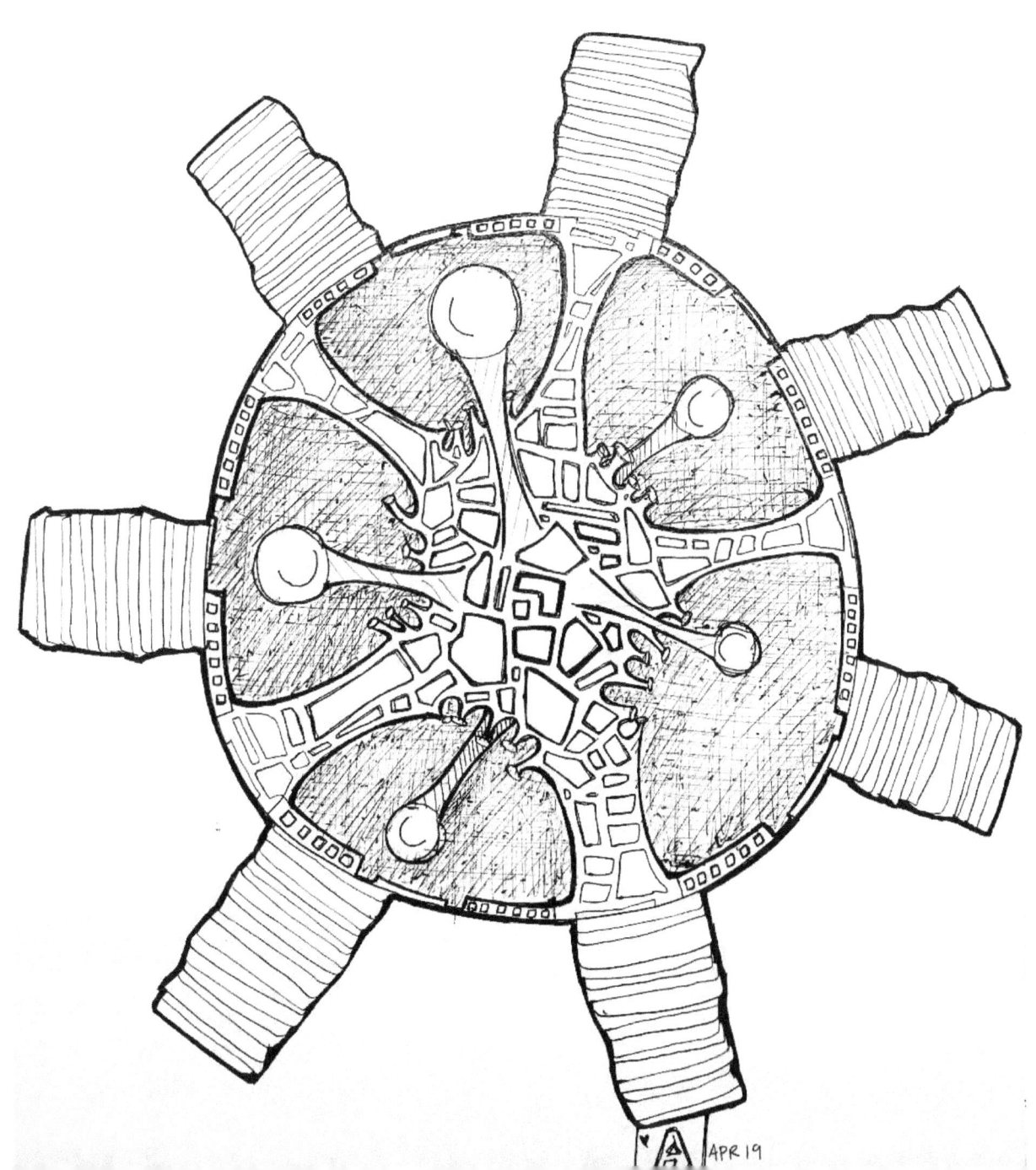

APR 19

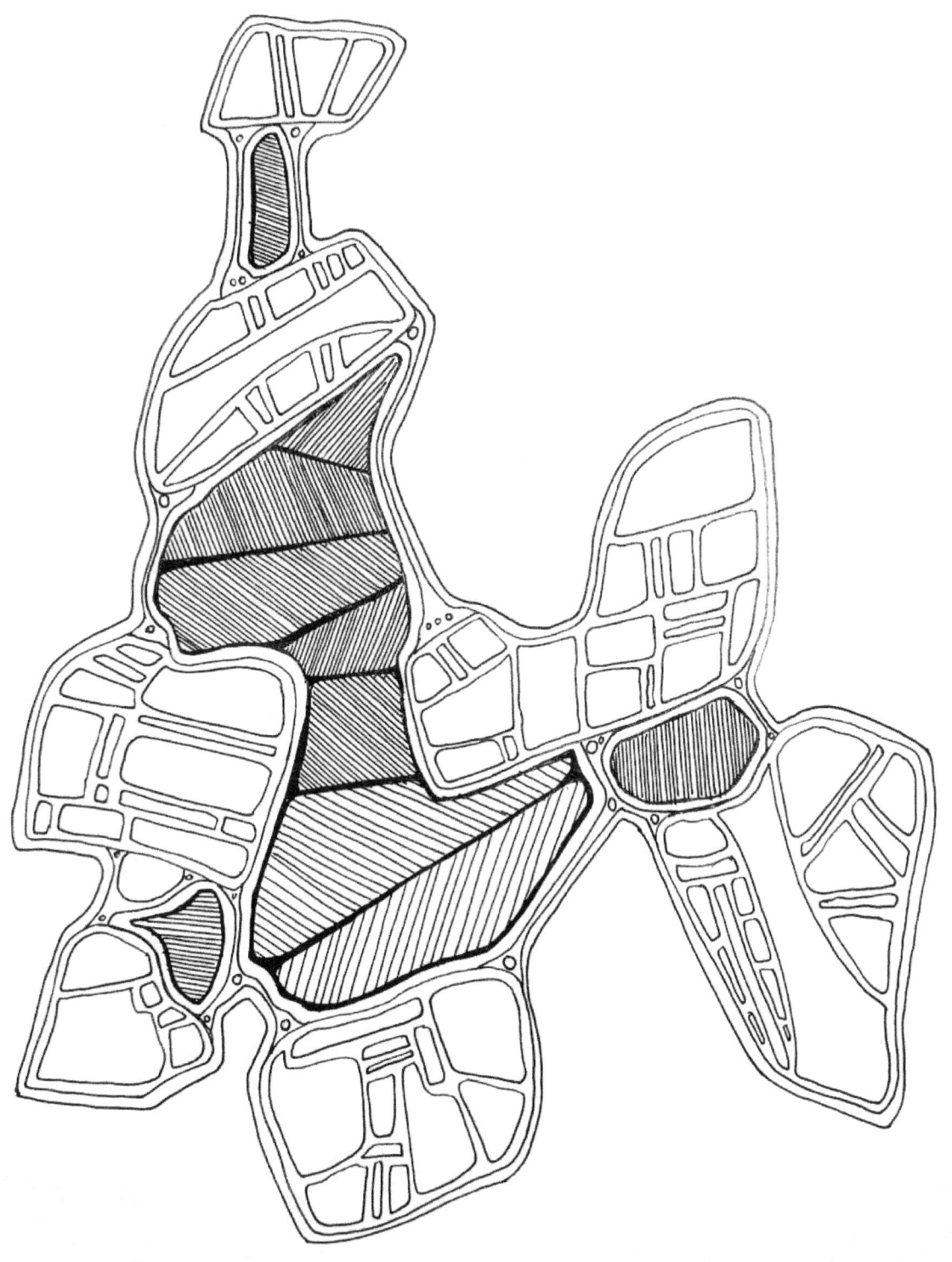

DEC 27
2020

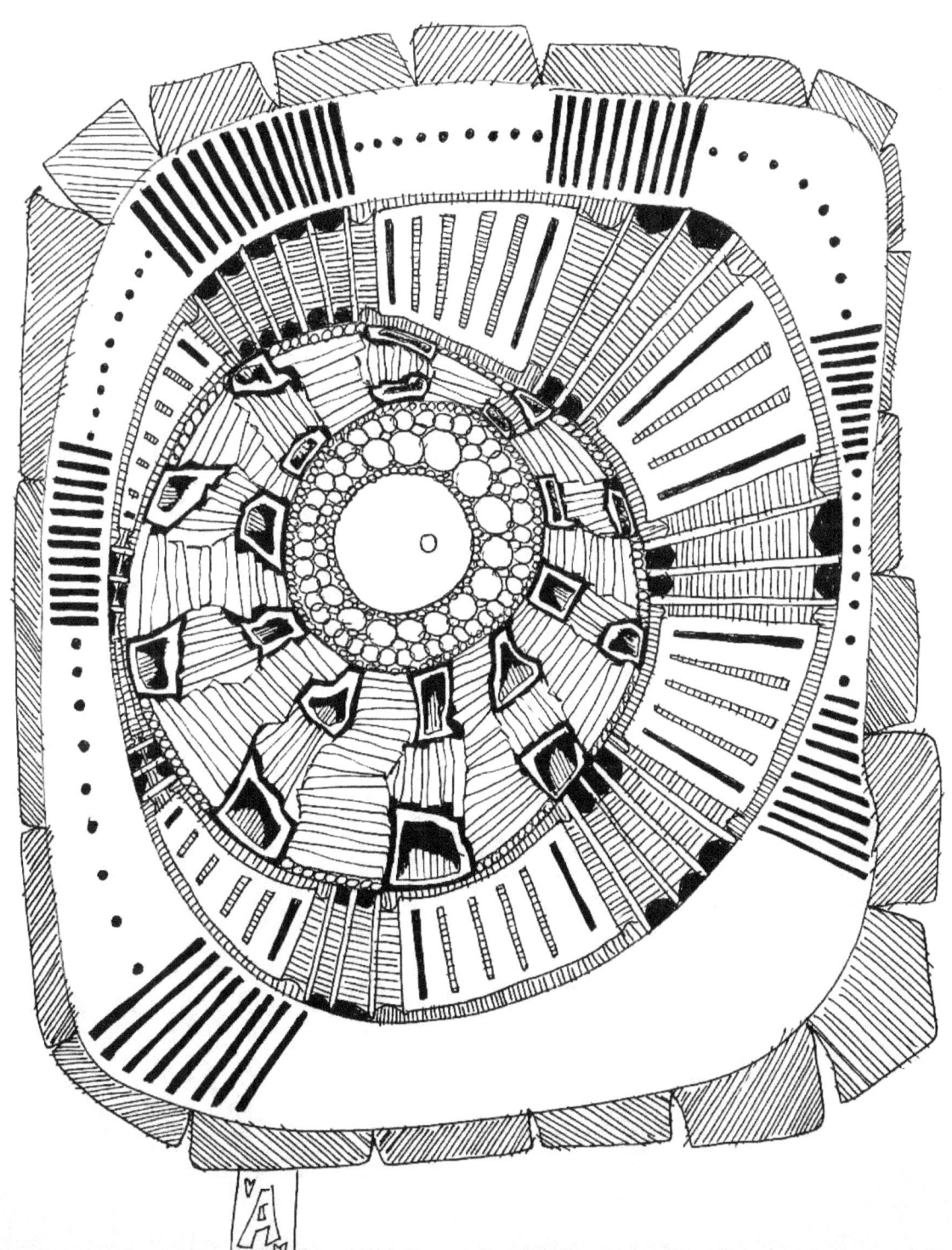

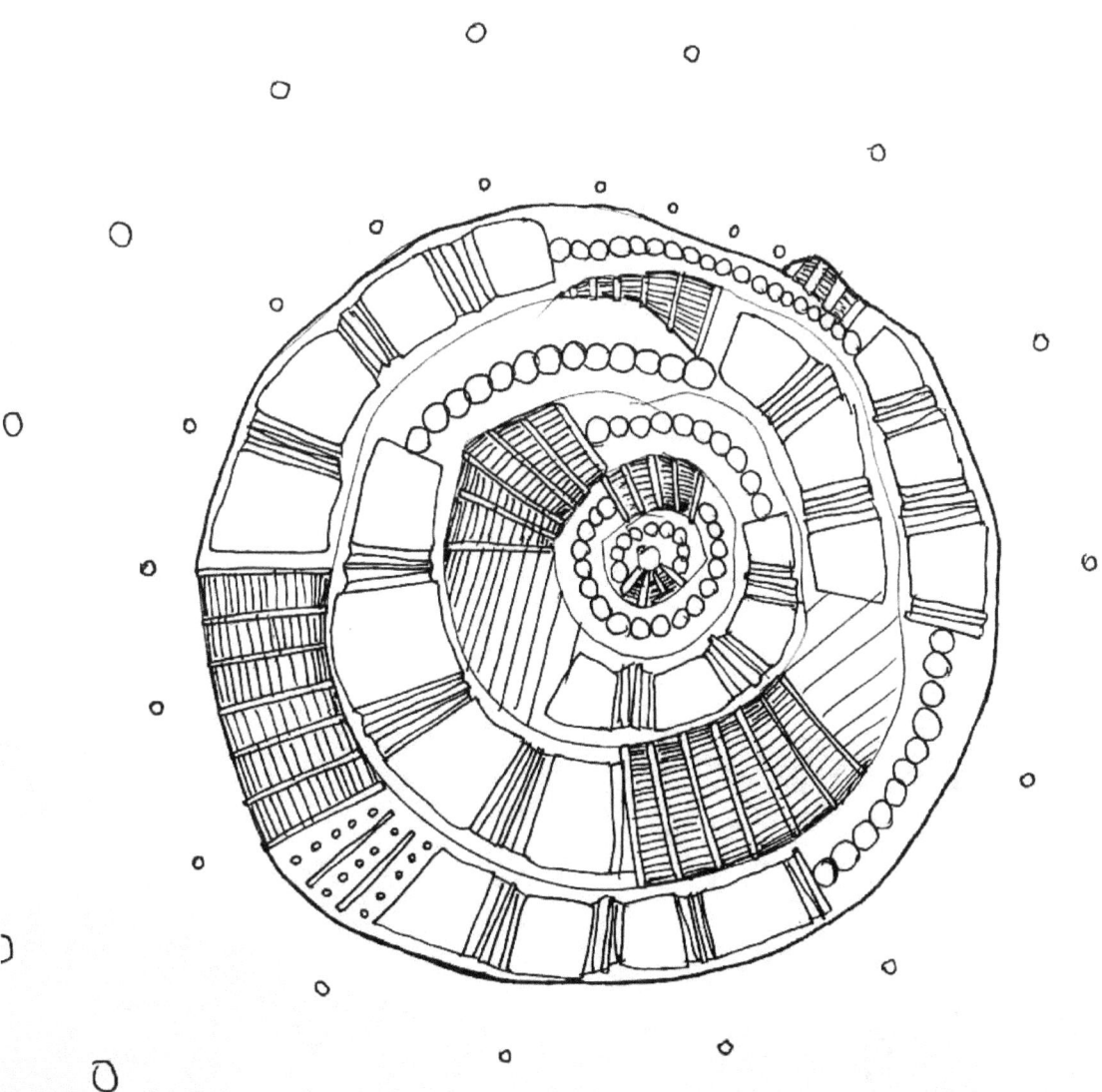

Draw 1, 2019

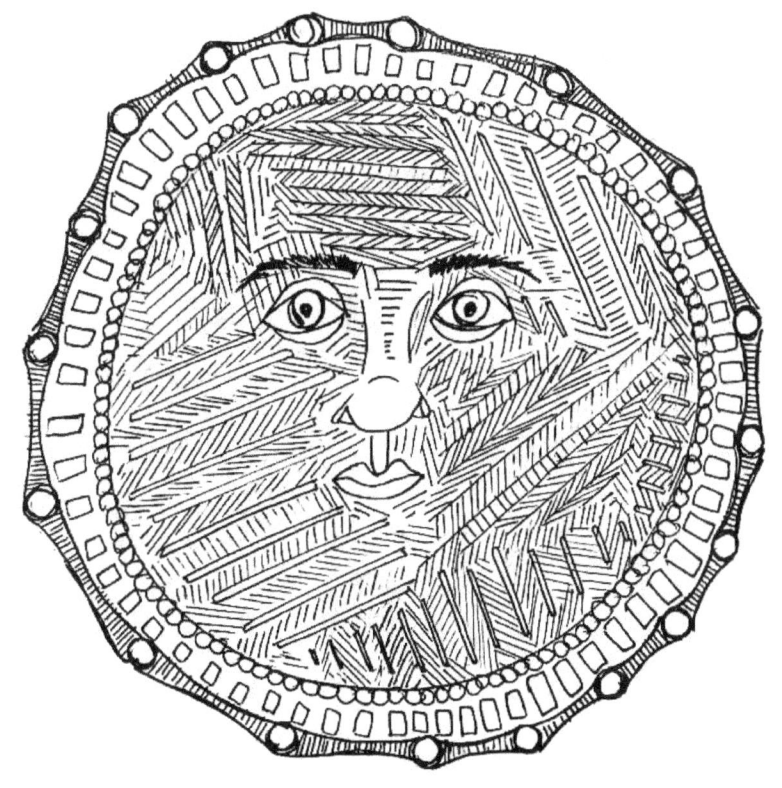

MARCH 31-2019

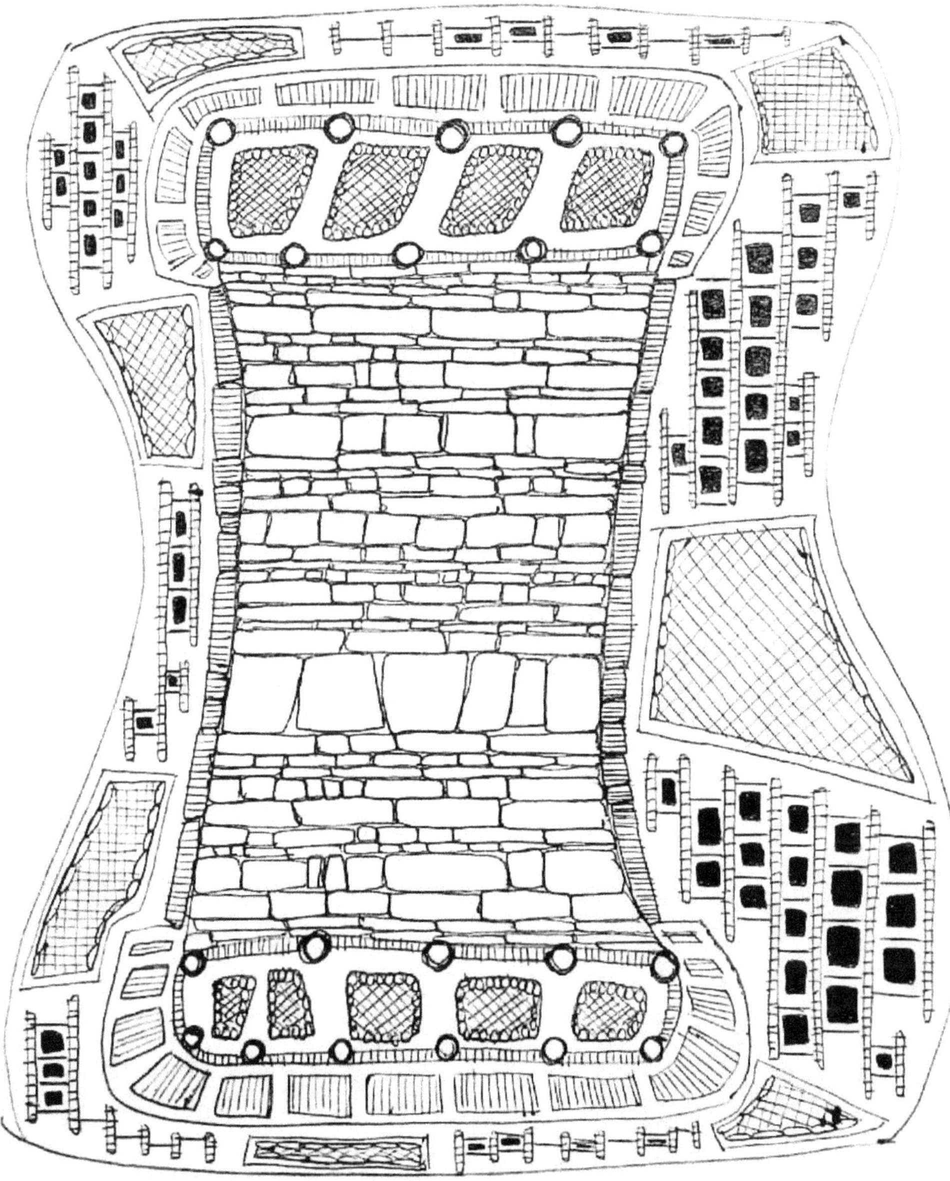

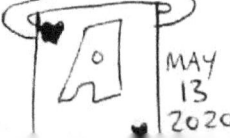

MAY
13
2020

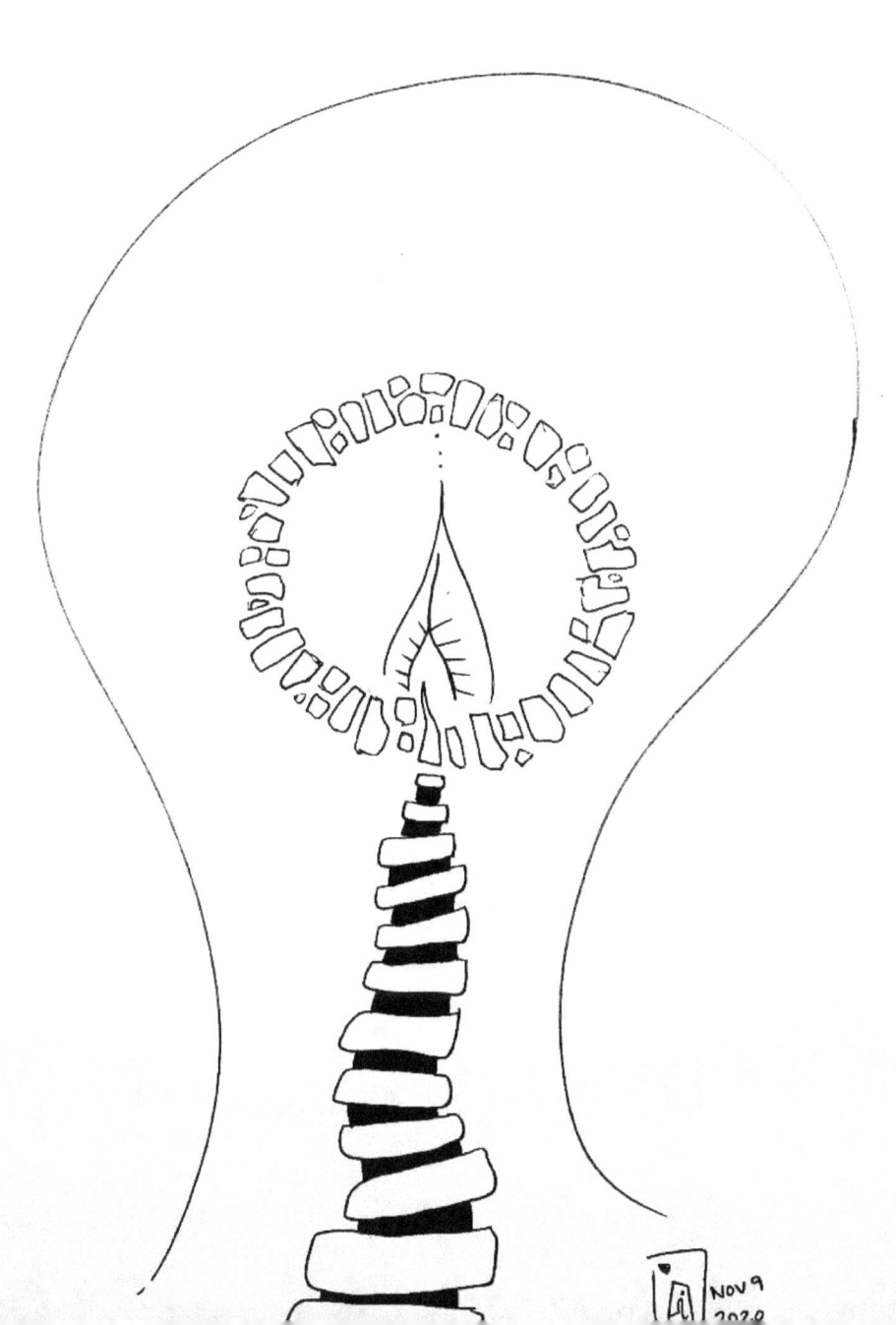

NOV 9
2020

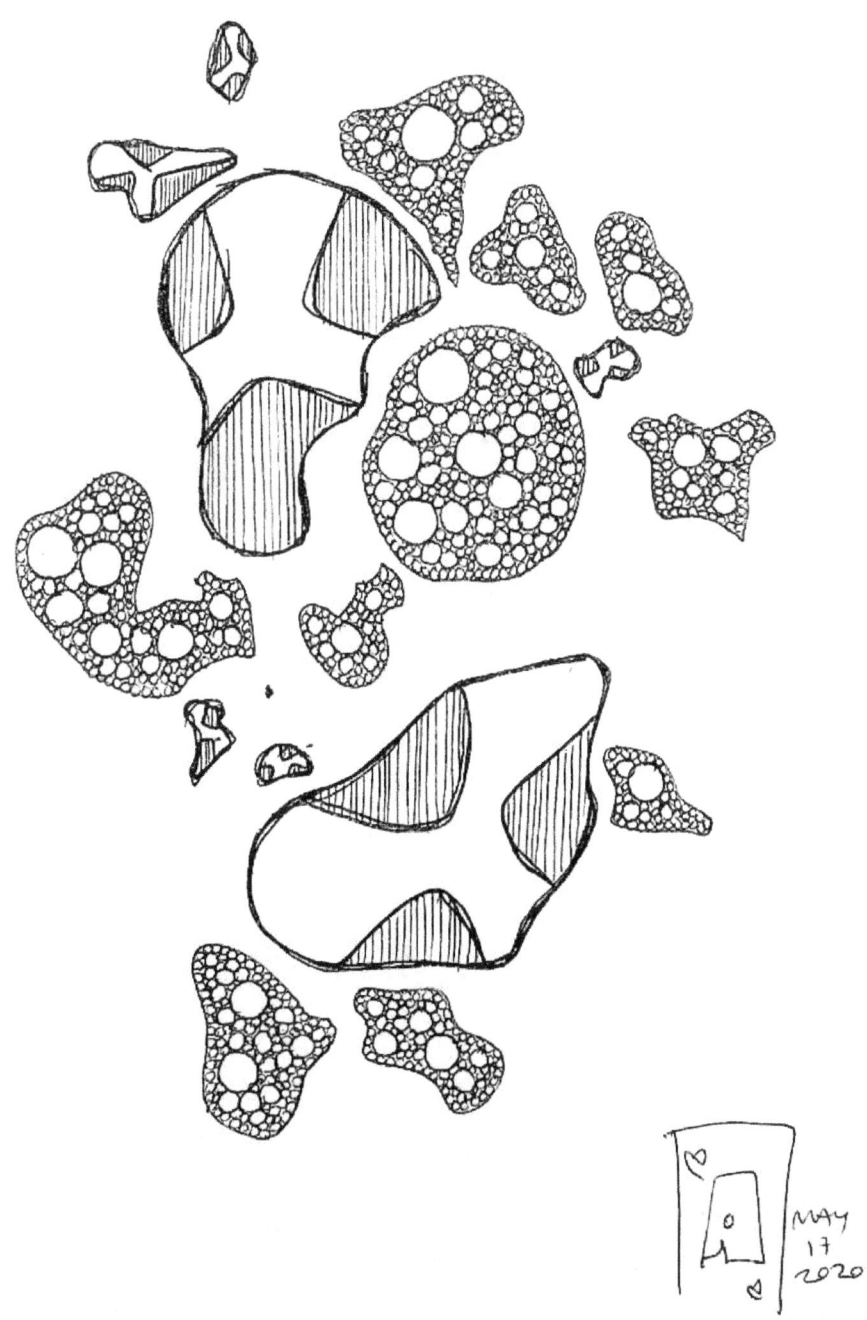

MAY
17
2020

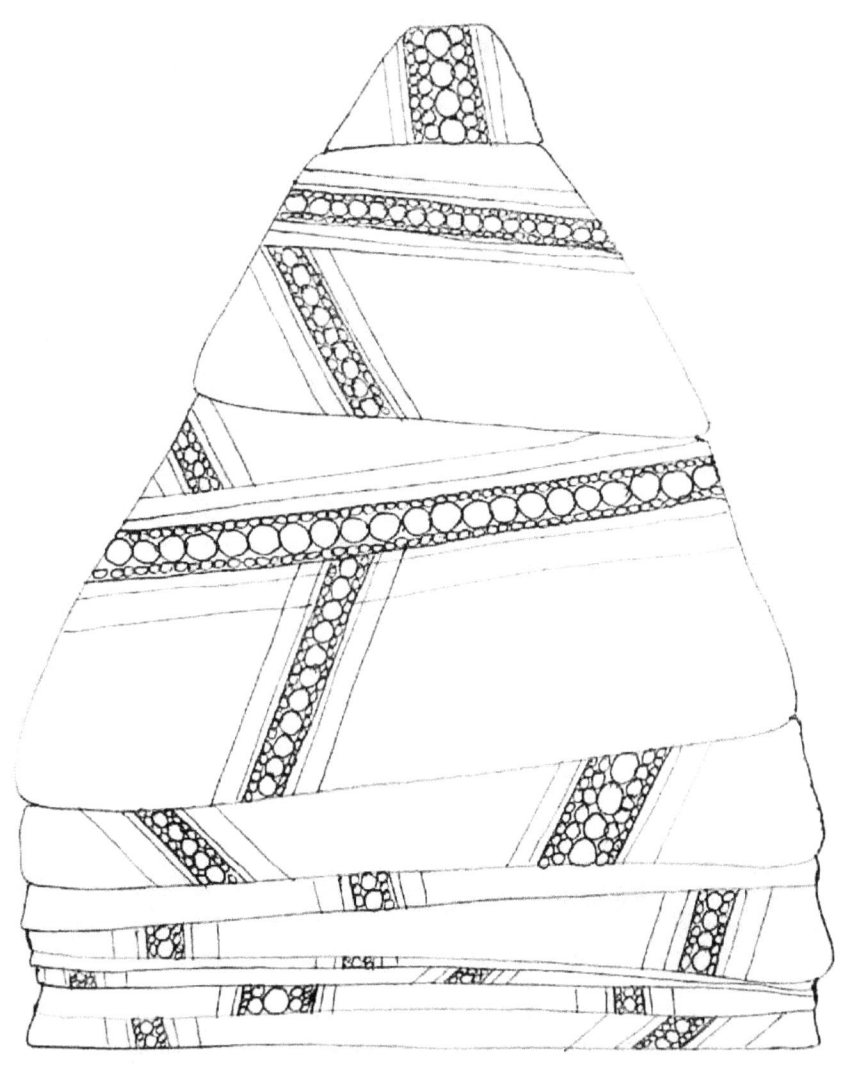

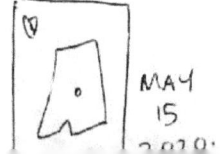
MAY
15
2020.

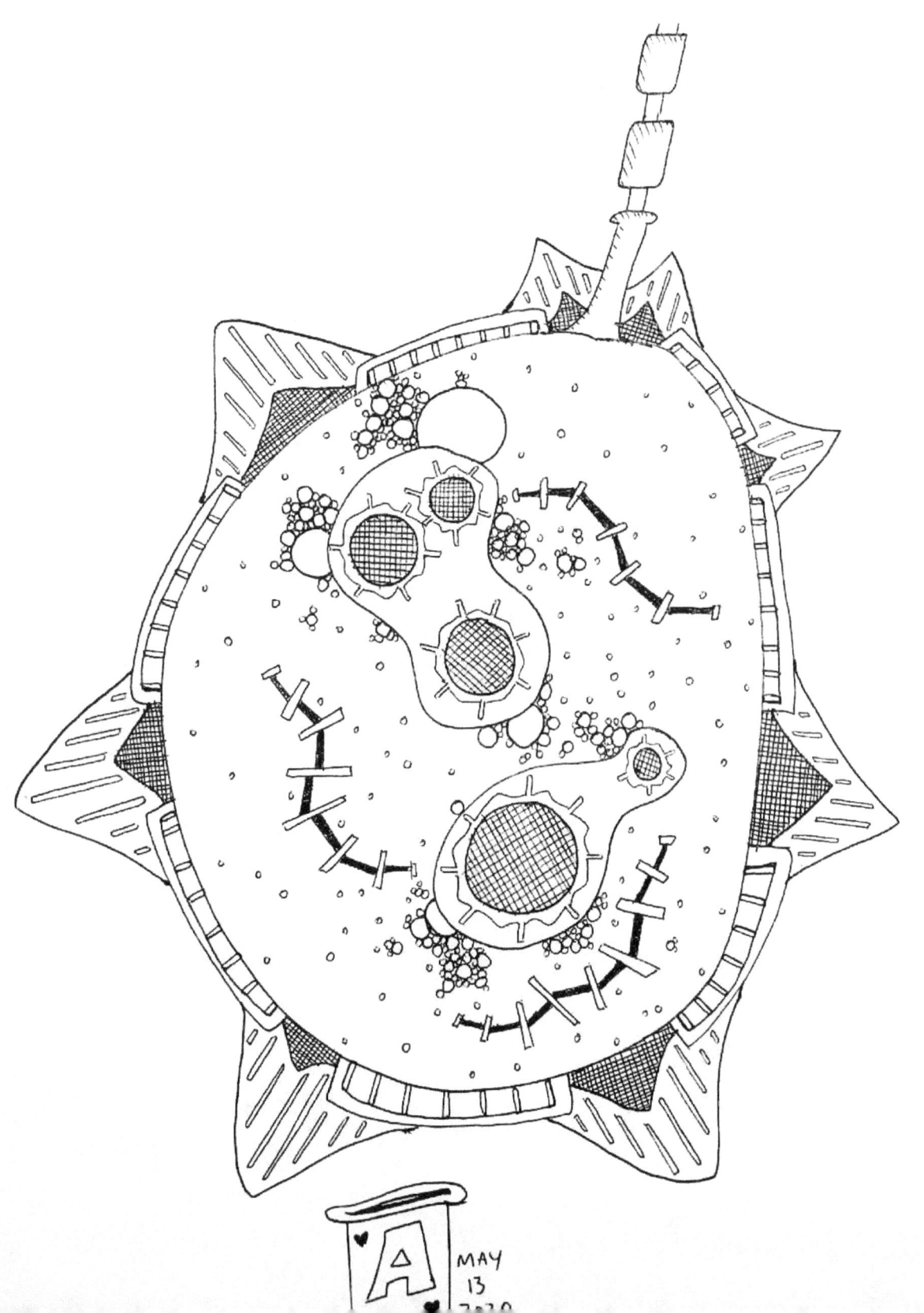

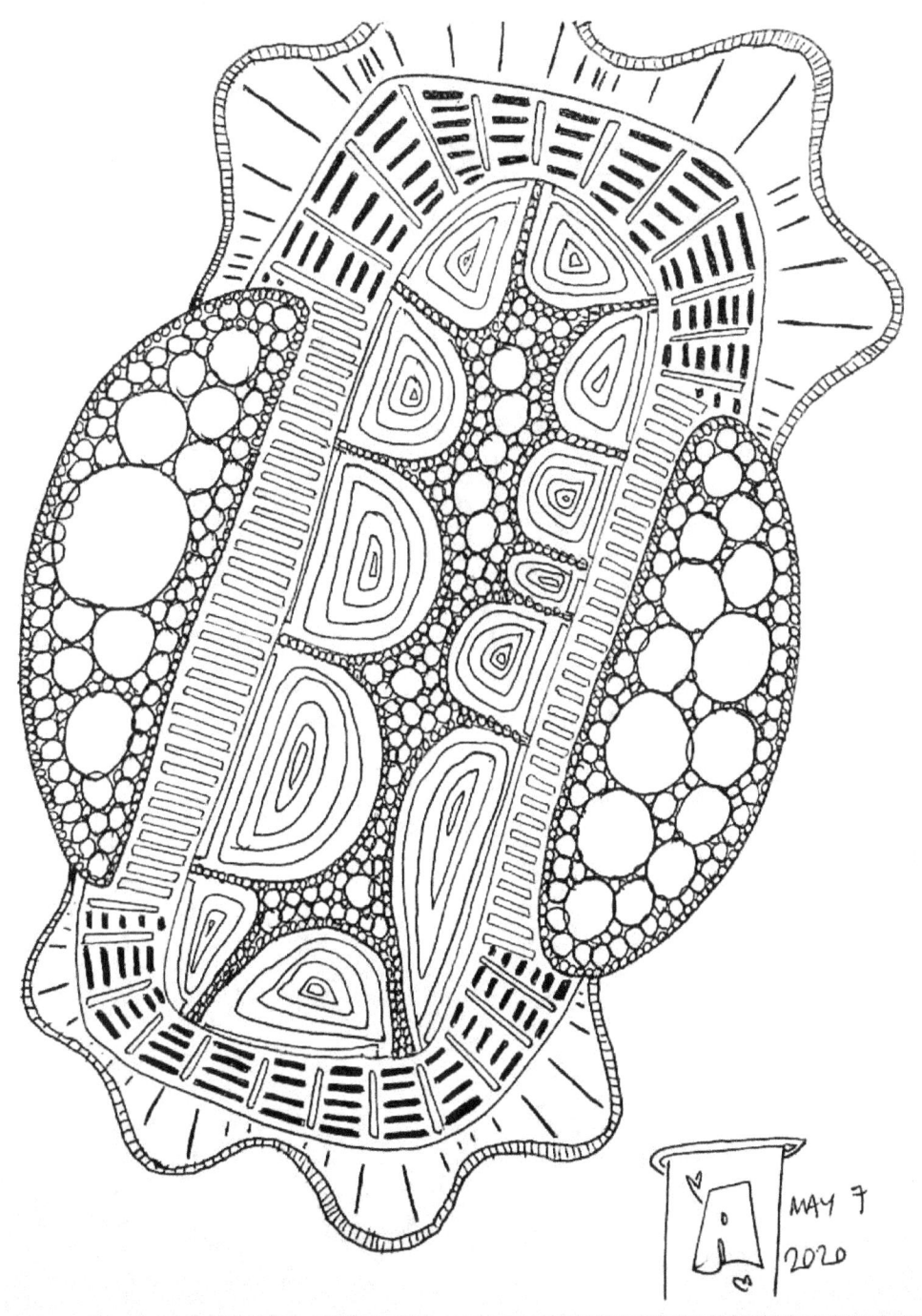

MAY 7
2020

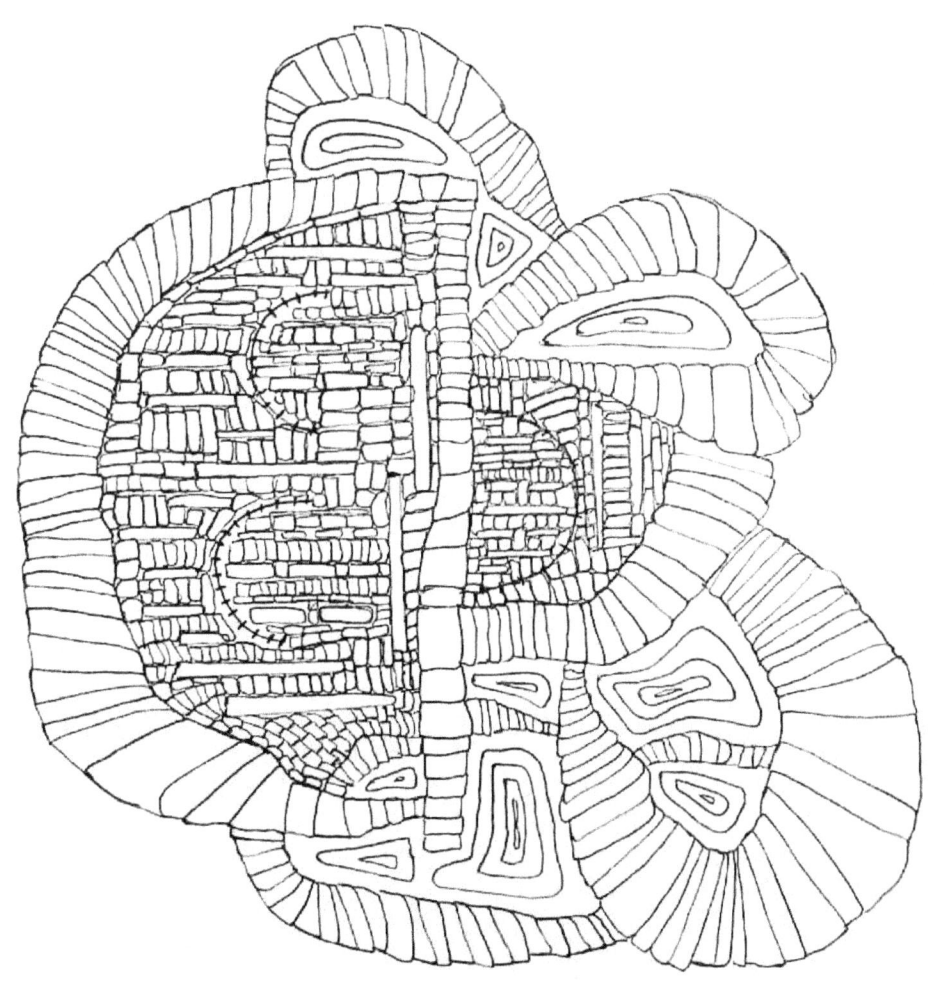

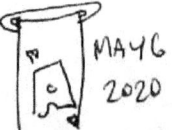 MAY6
2020

EXTRATERRESTRIAL

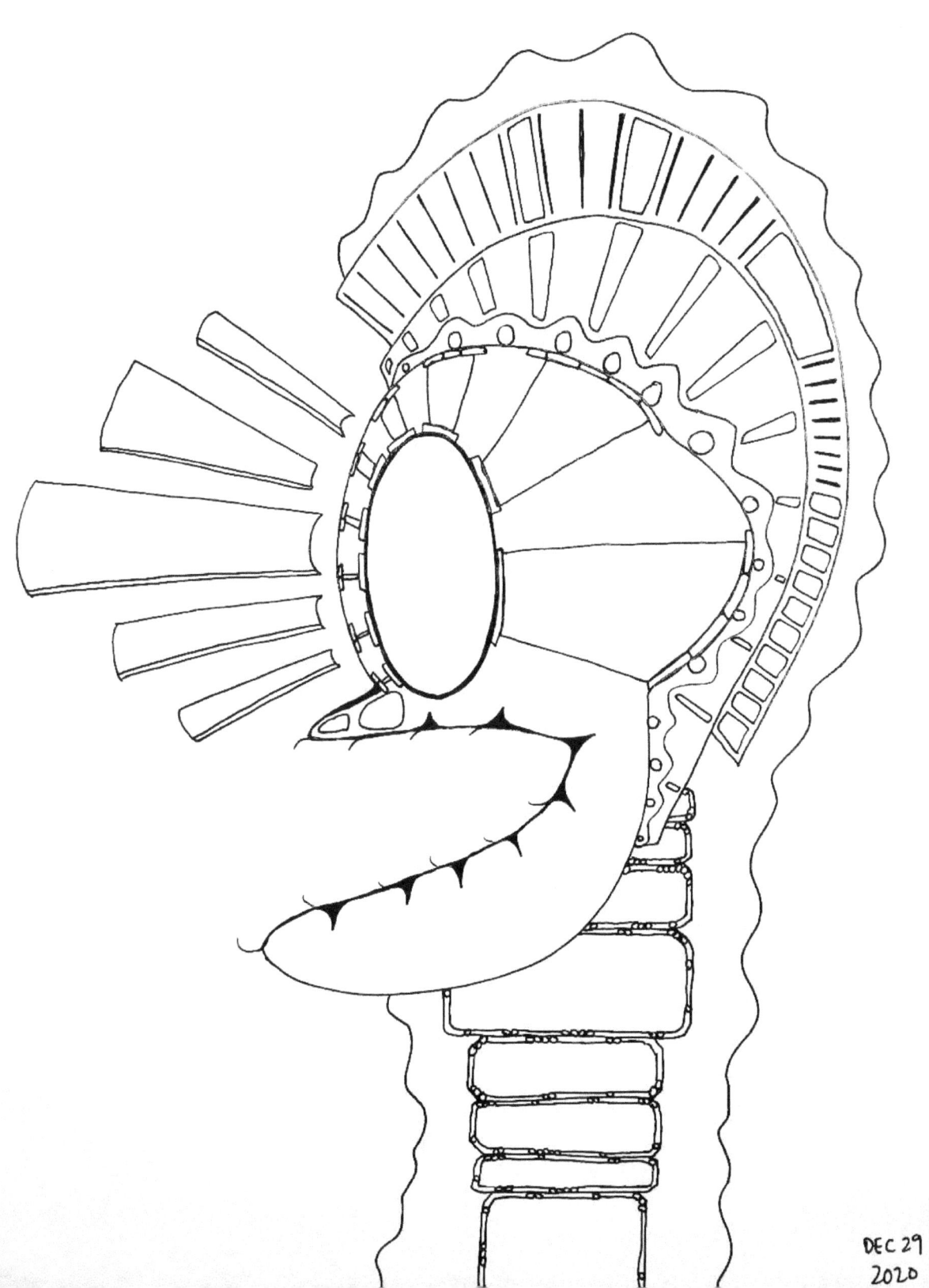

DEC 29
2020

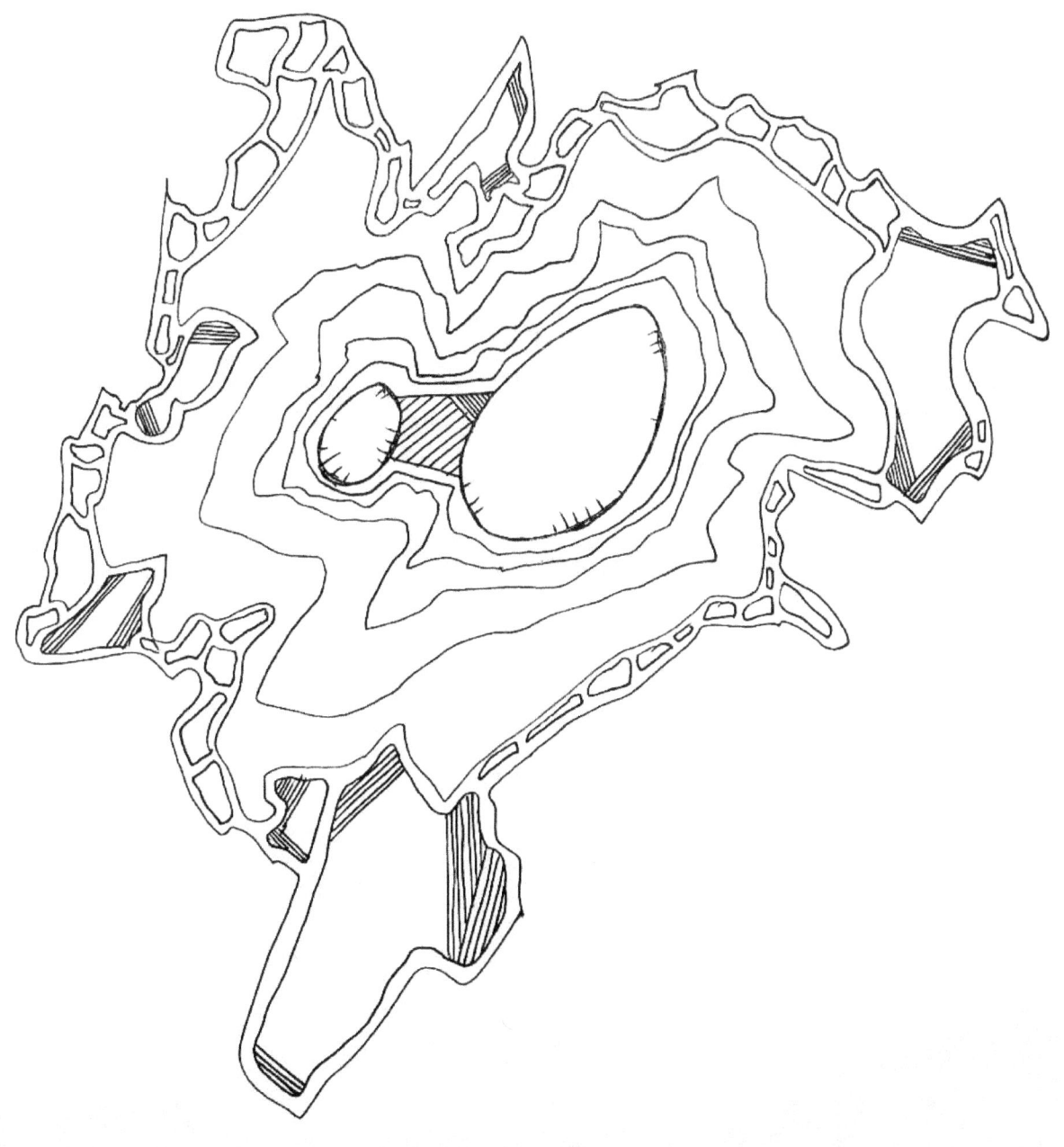

JAN 8
2021

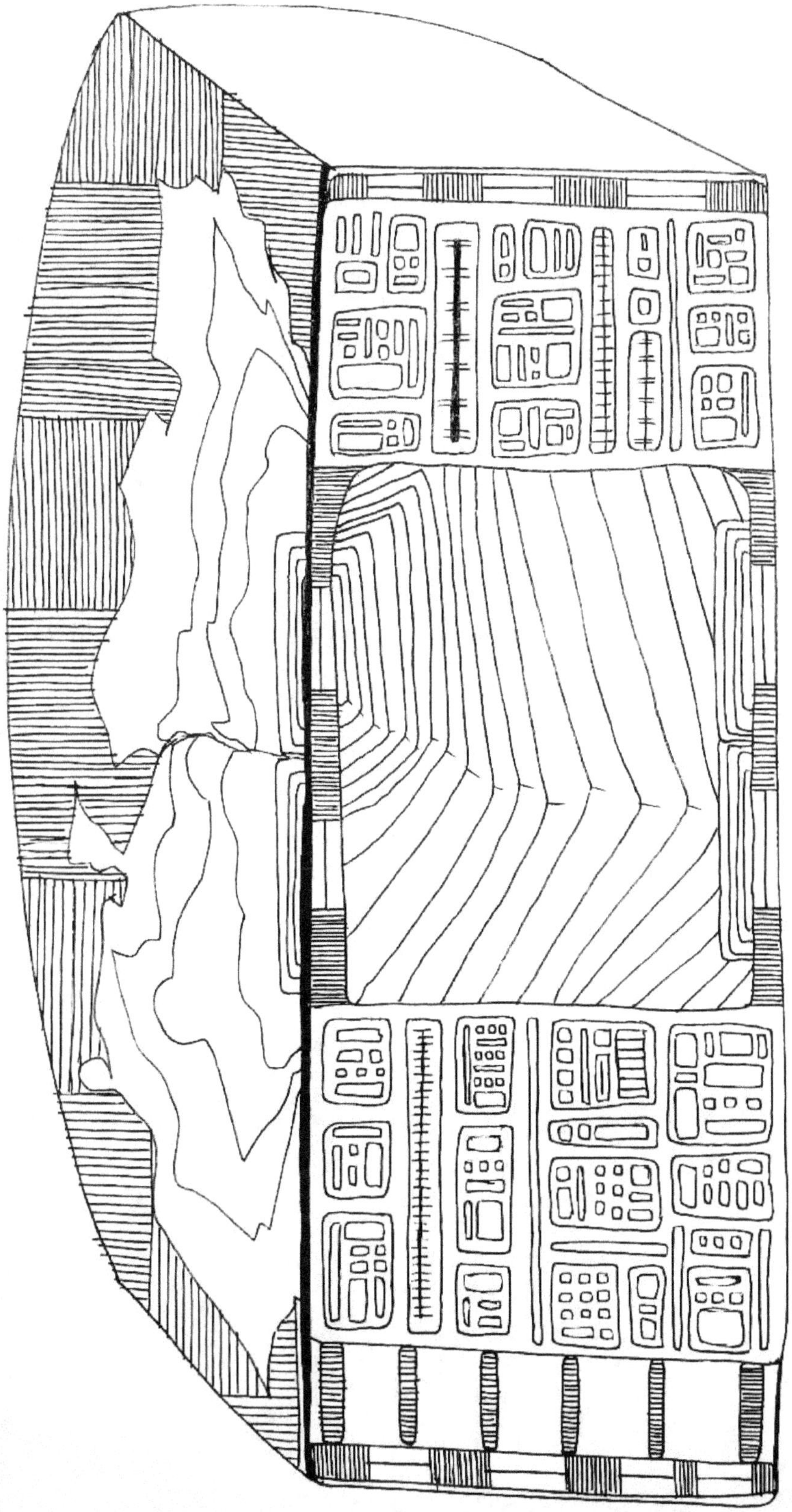

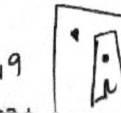

JAN 9

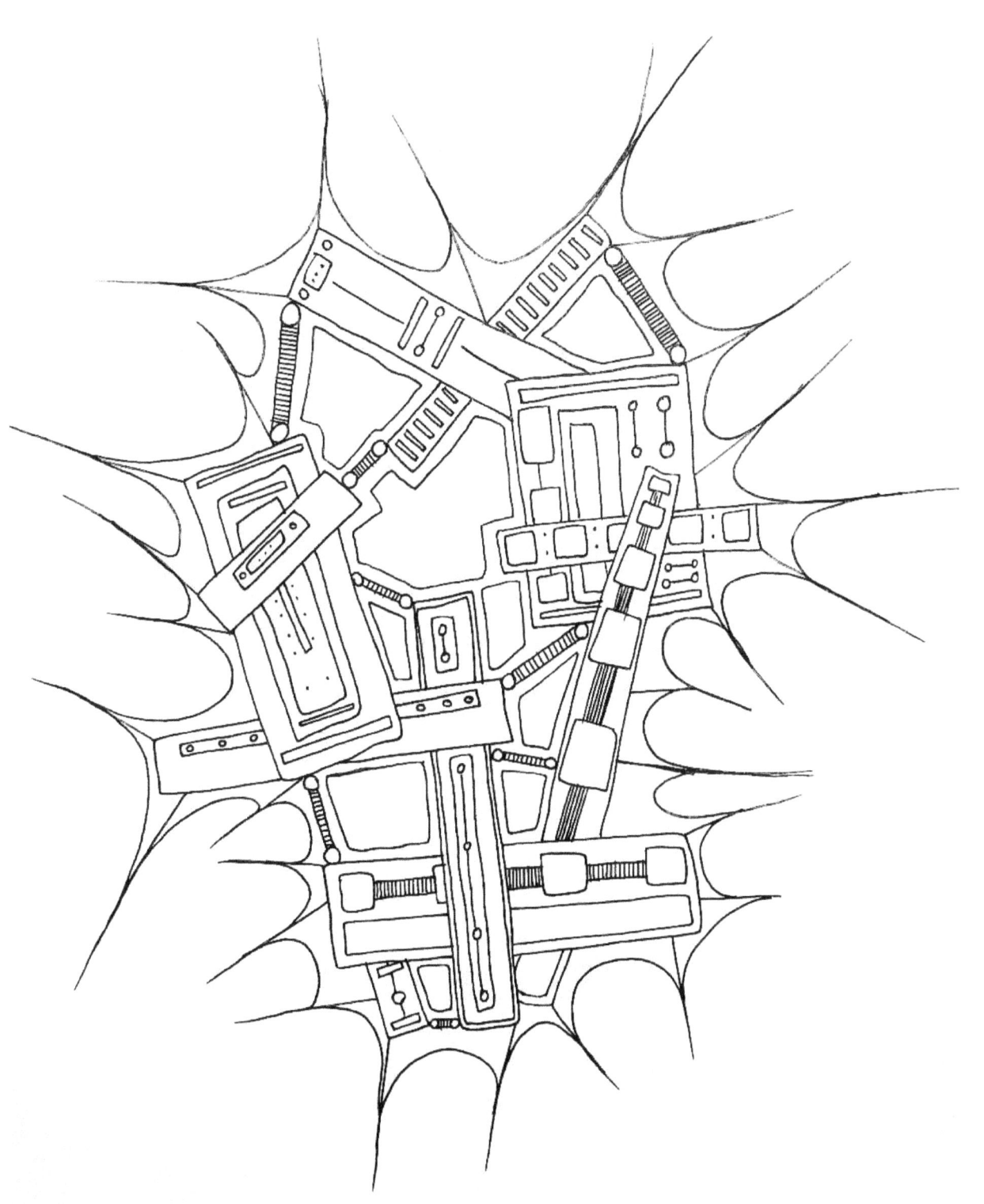

DEC19

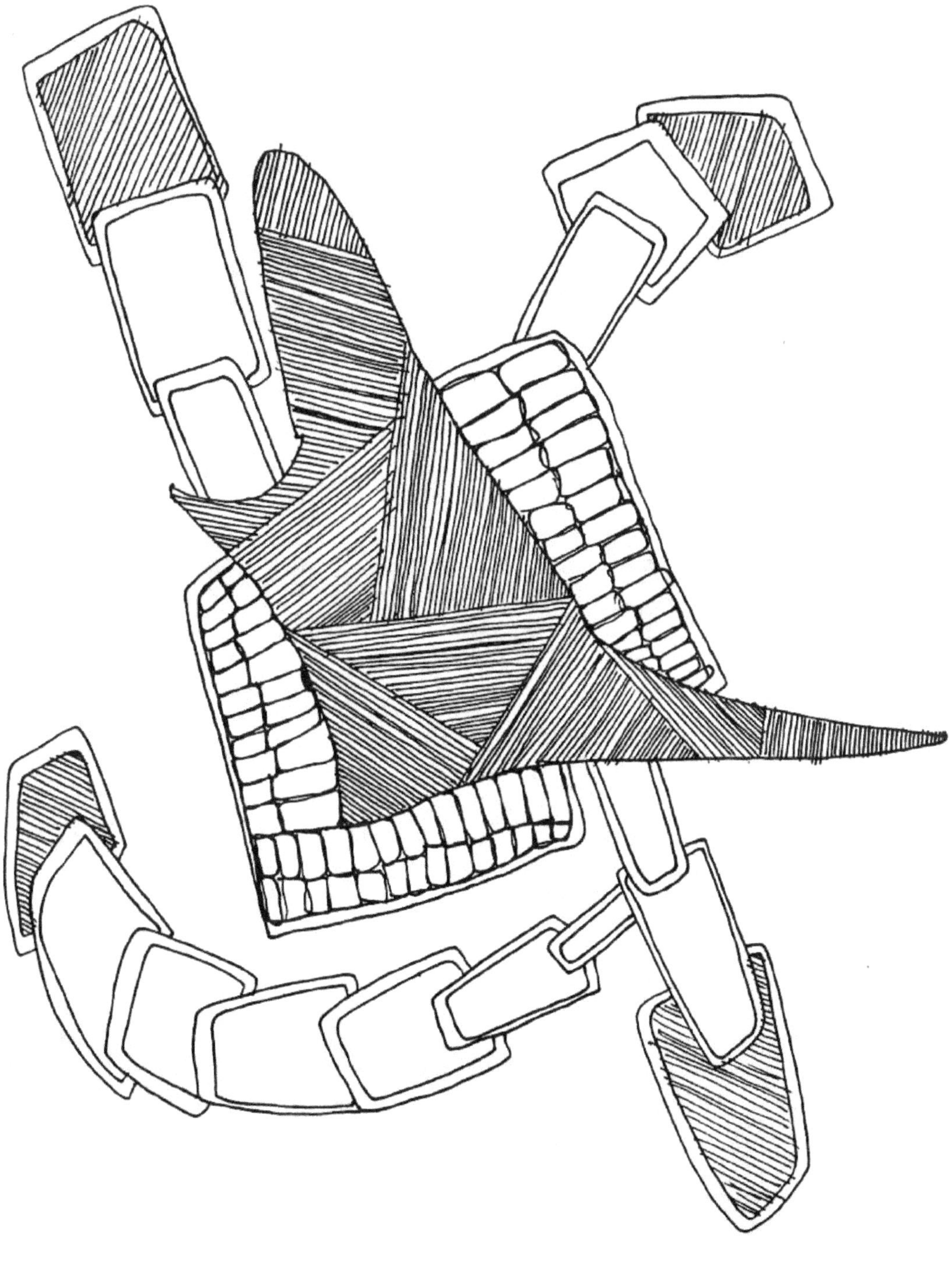

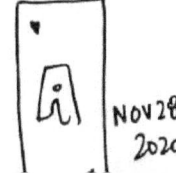

NOV 28
2020

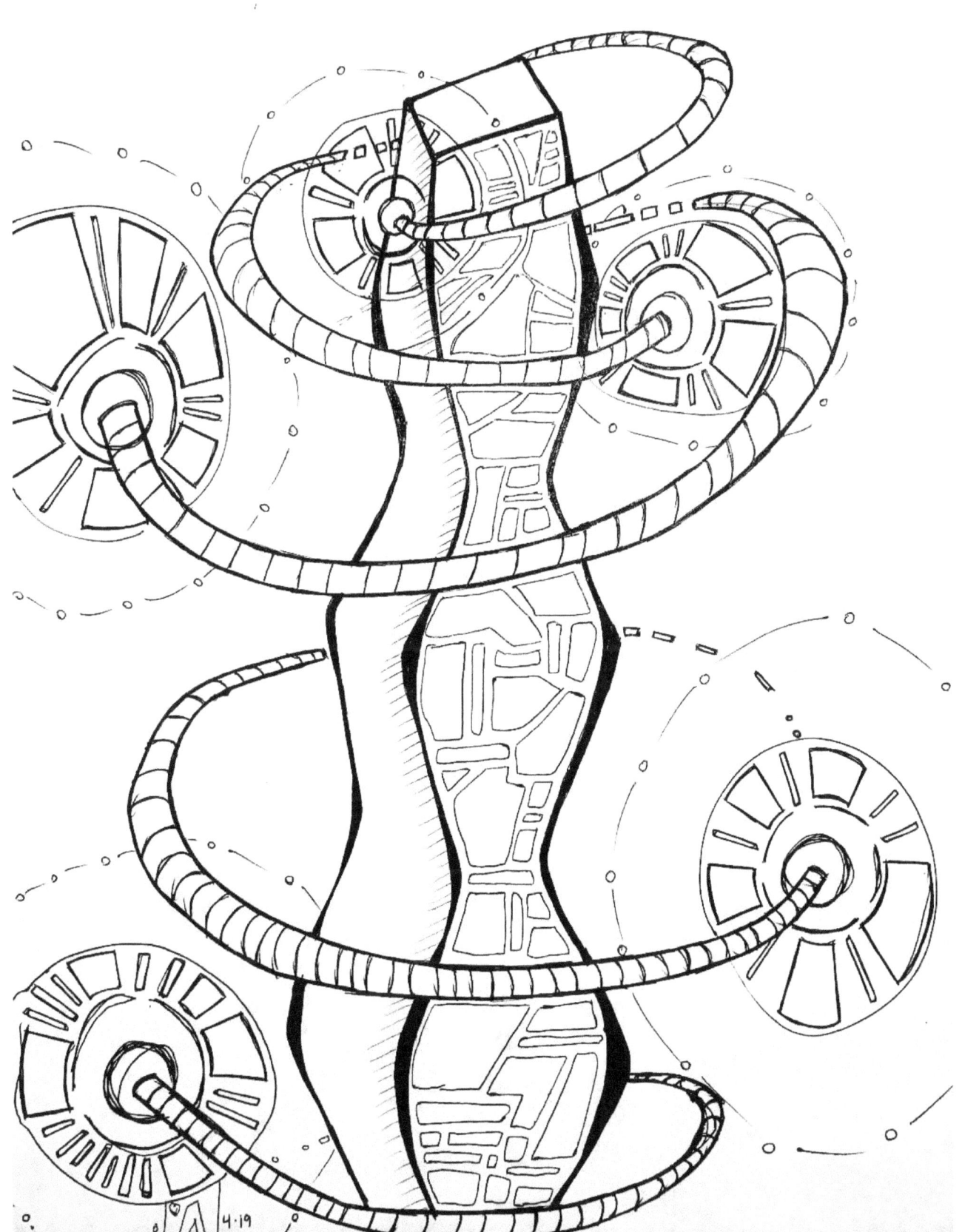

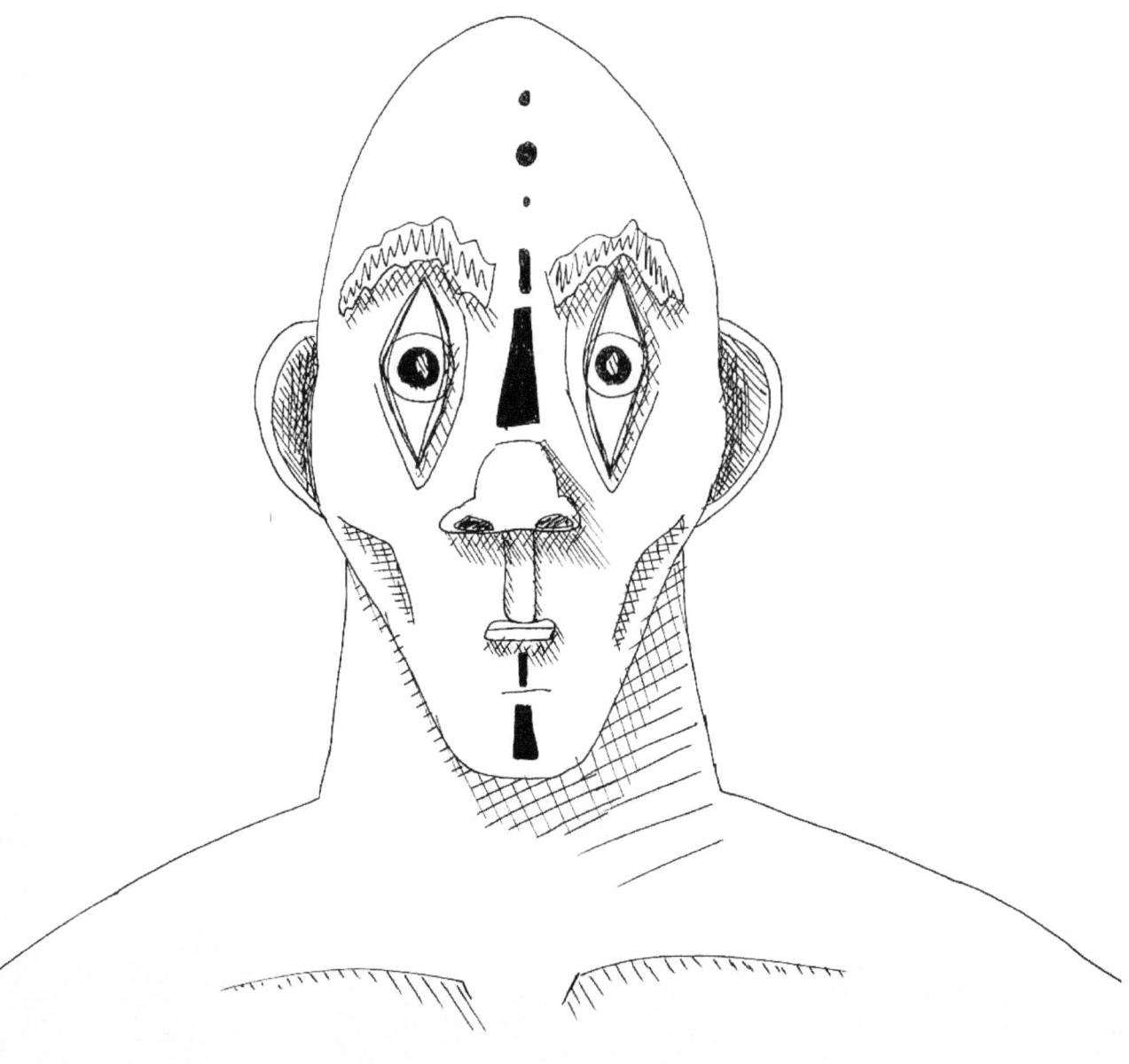

JAN 1

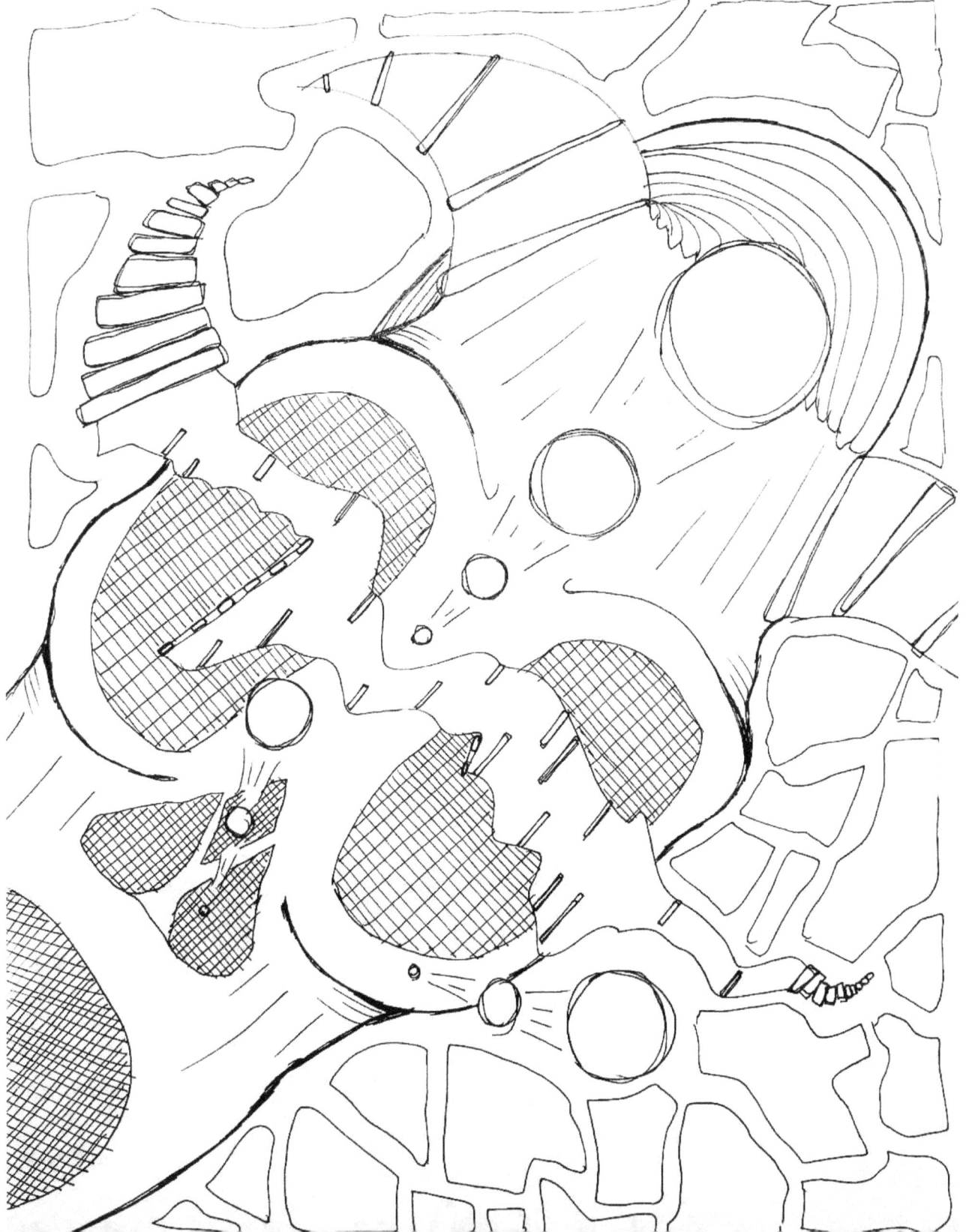

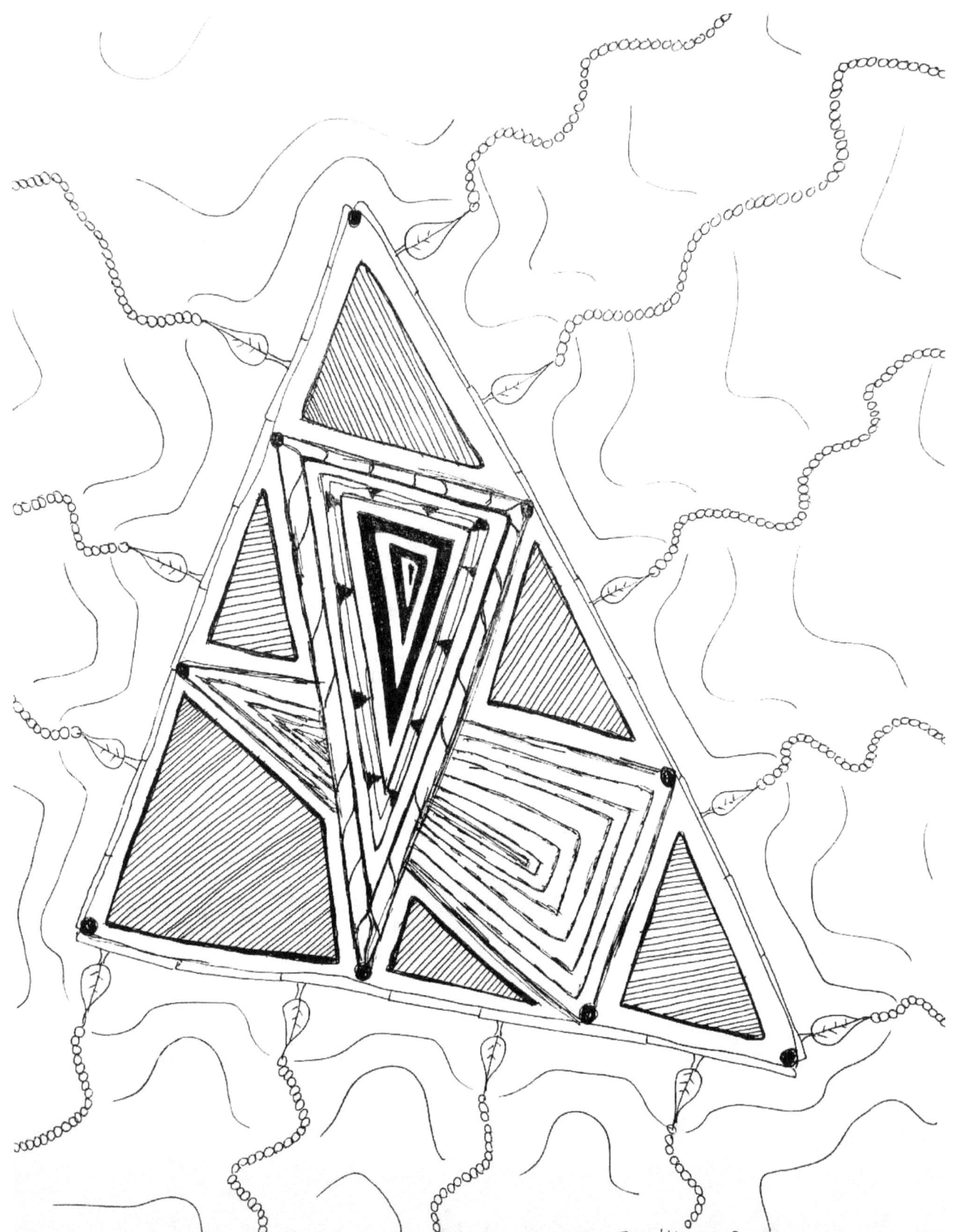

Feb 14 2019

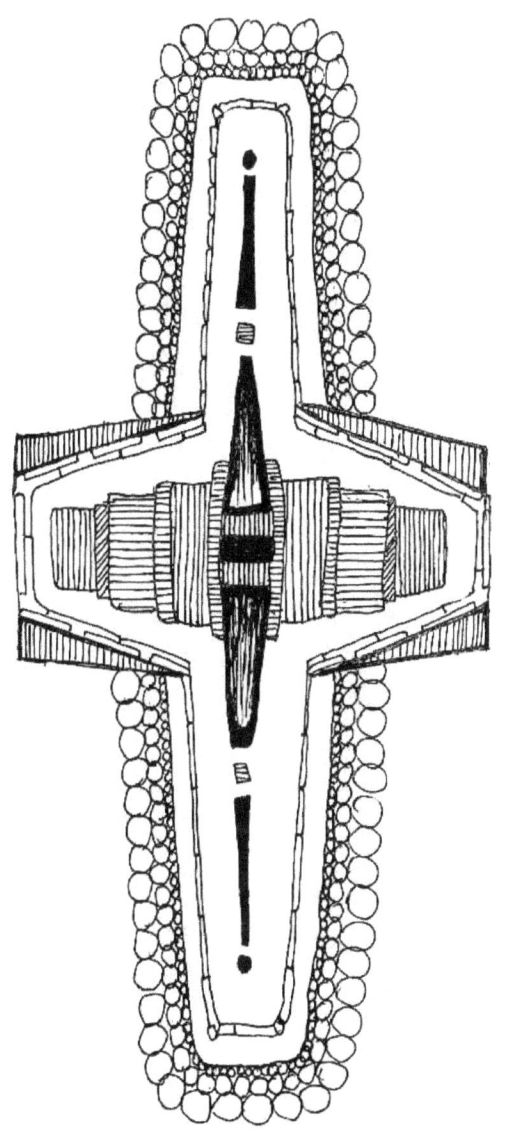

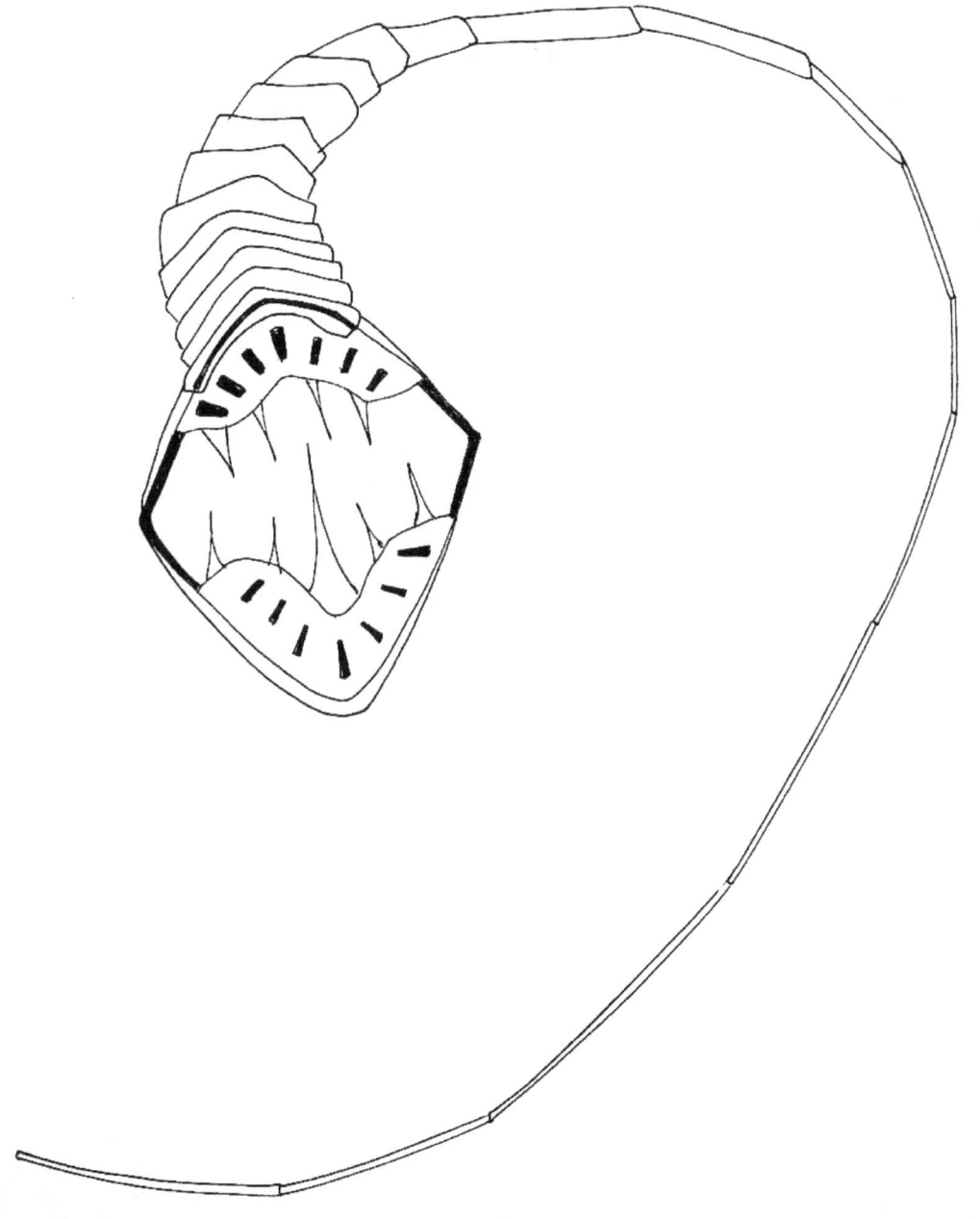

FEB18-2019

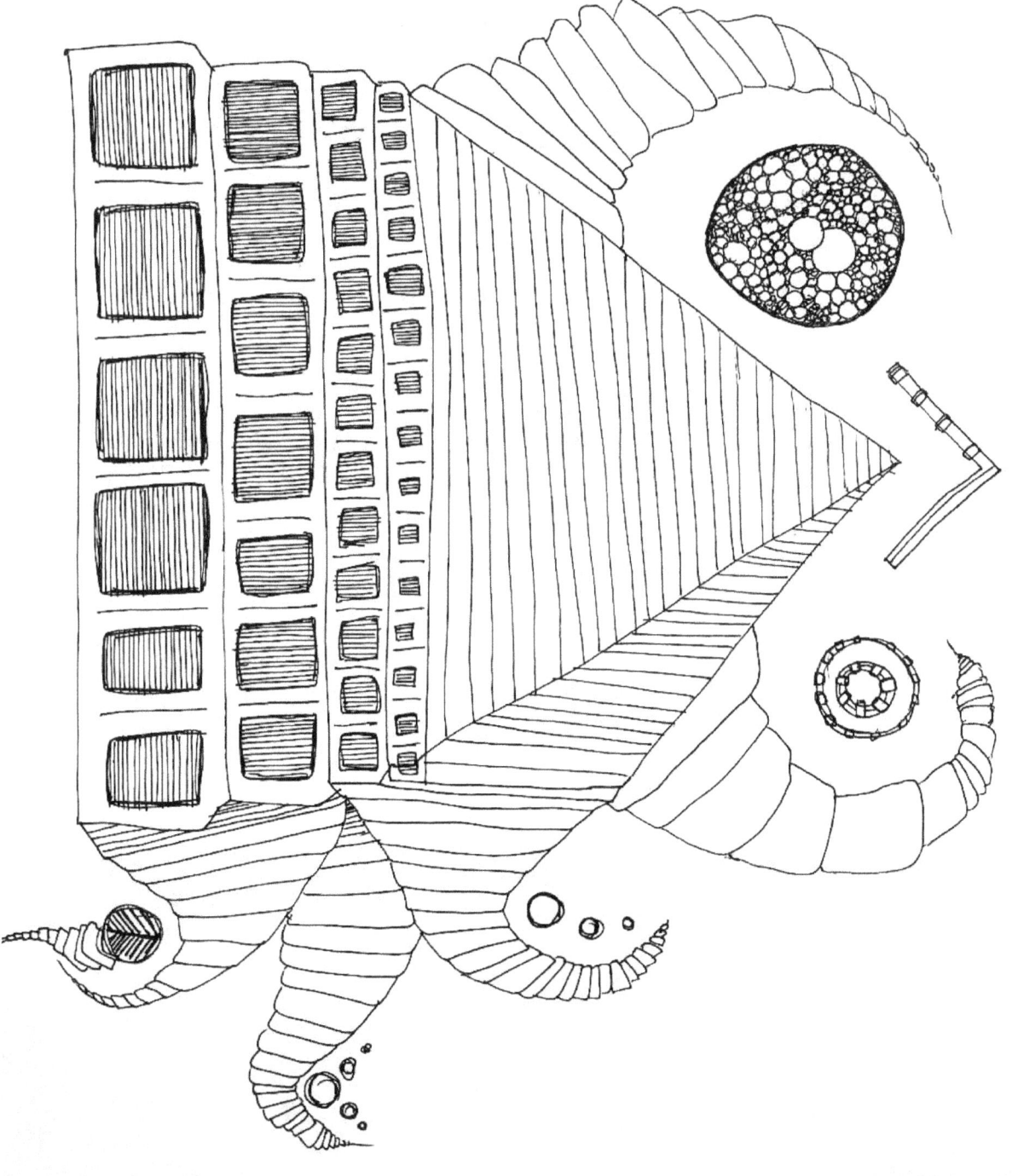

Feb 15 - 2019

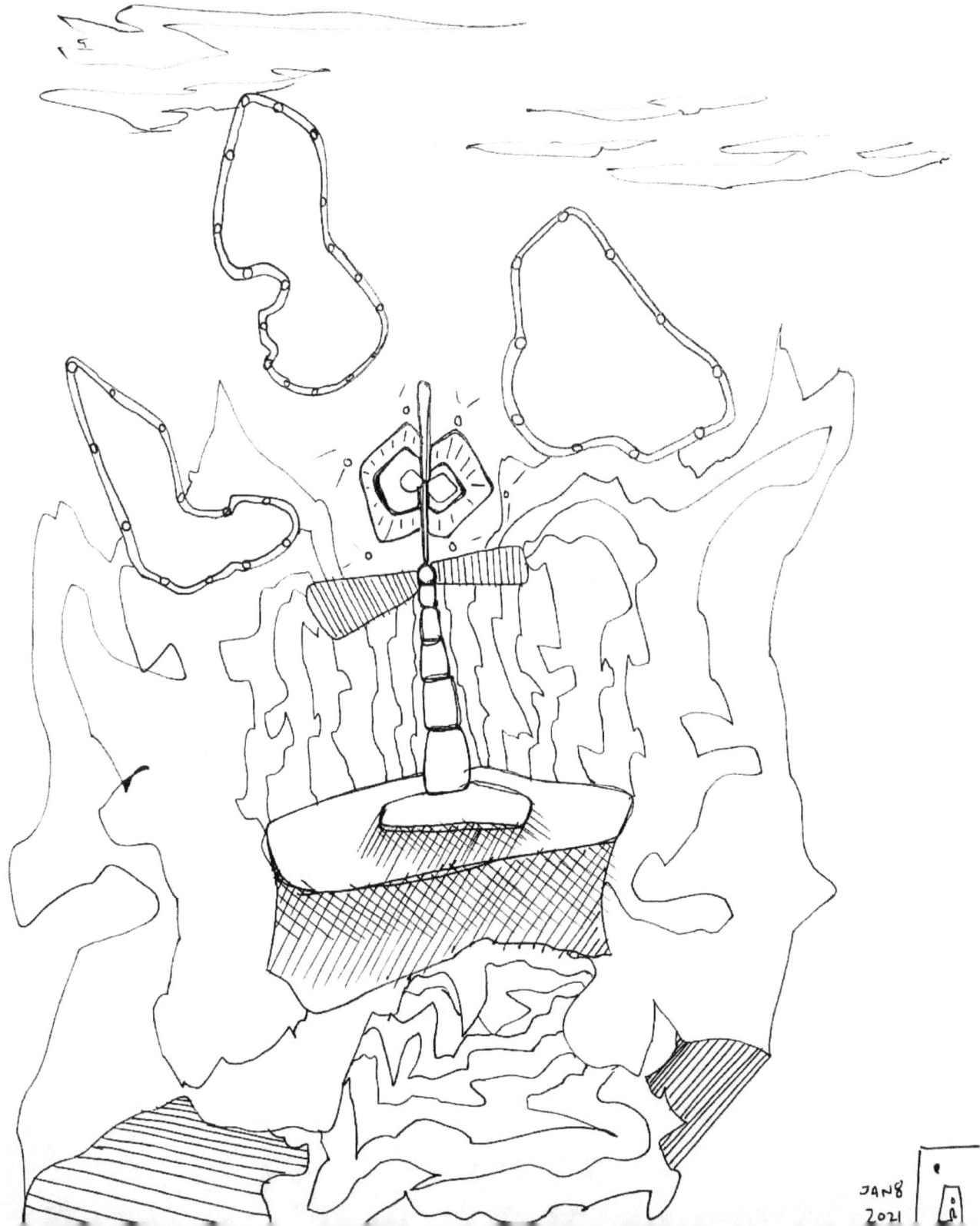

JAN 8
2021

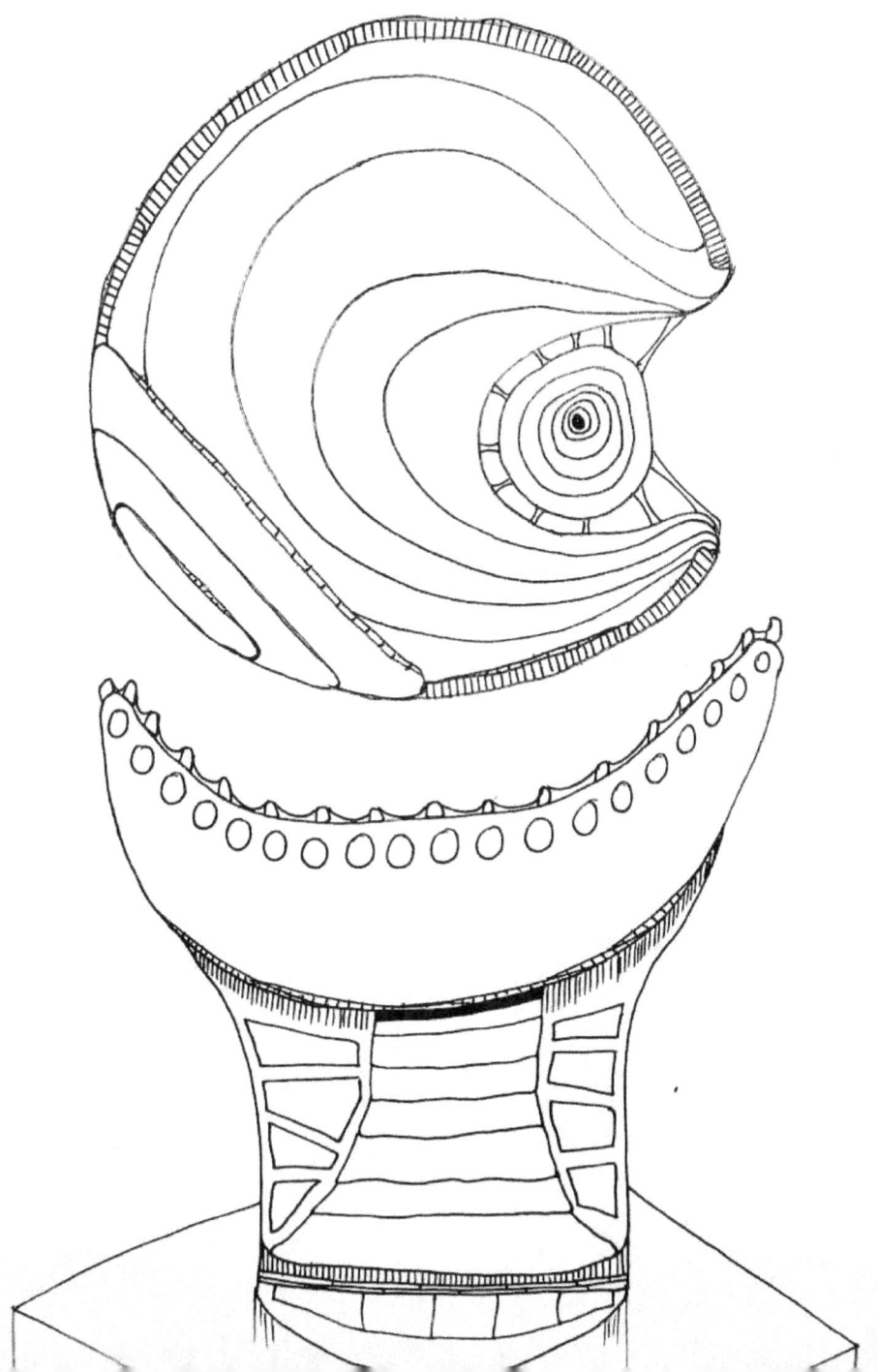

DEC19

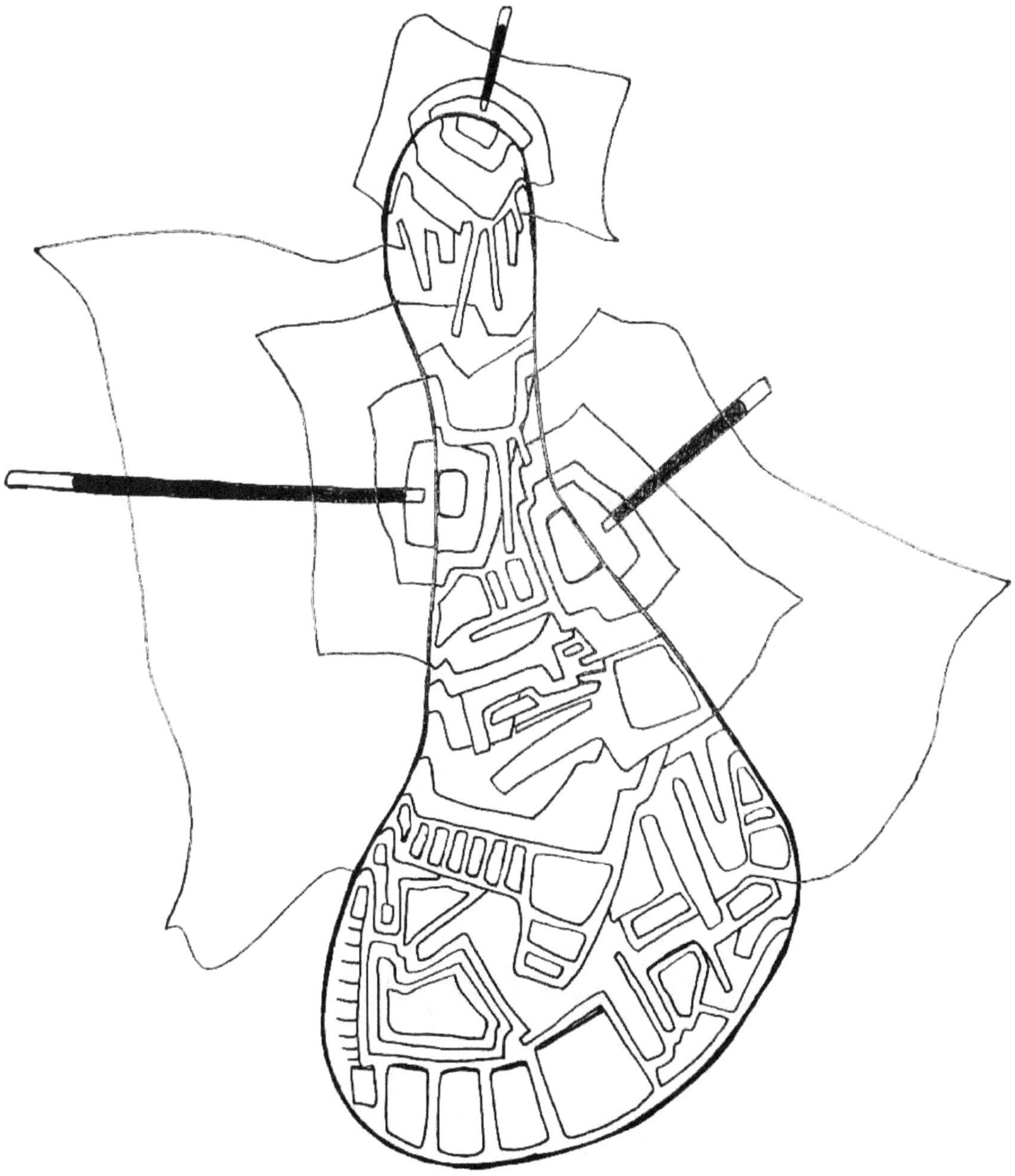

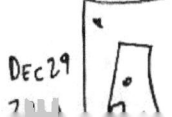

DEC 29

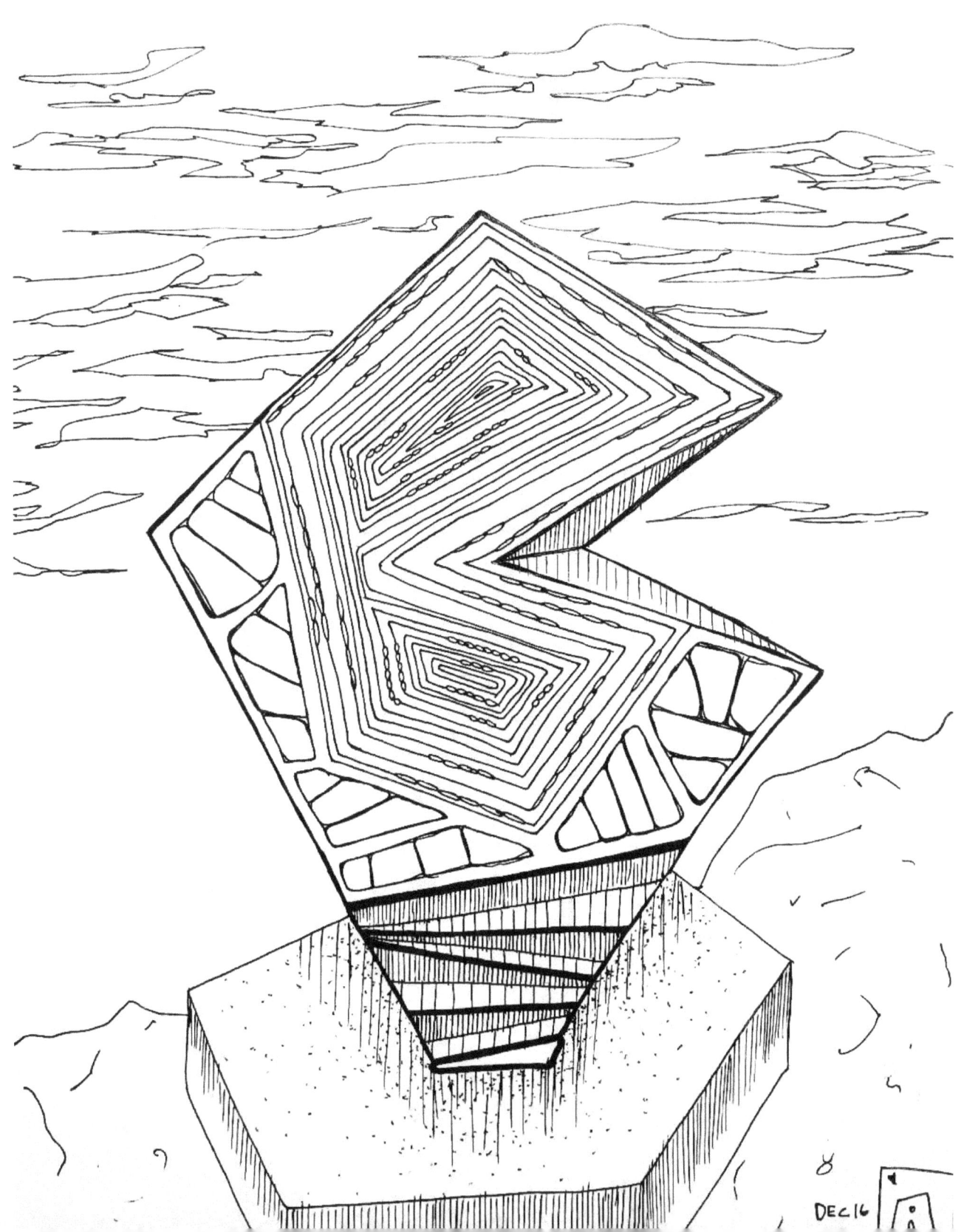

DEC 16

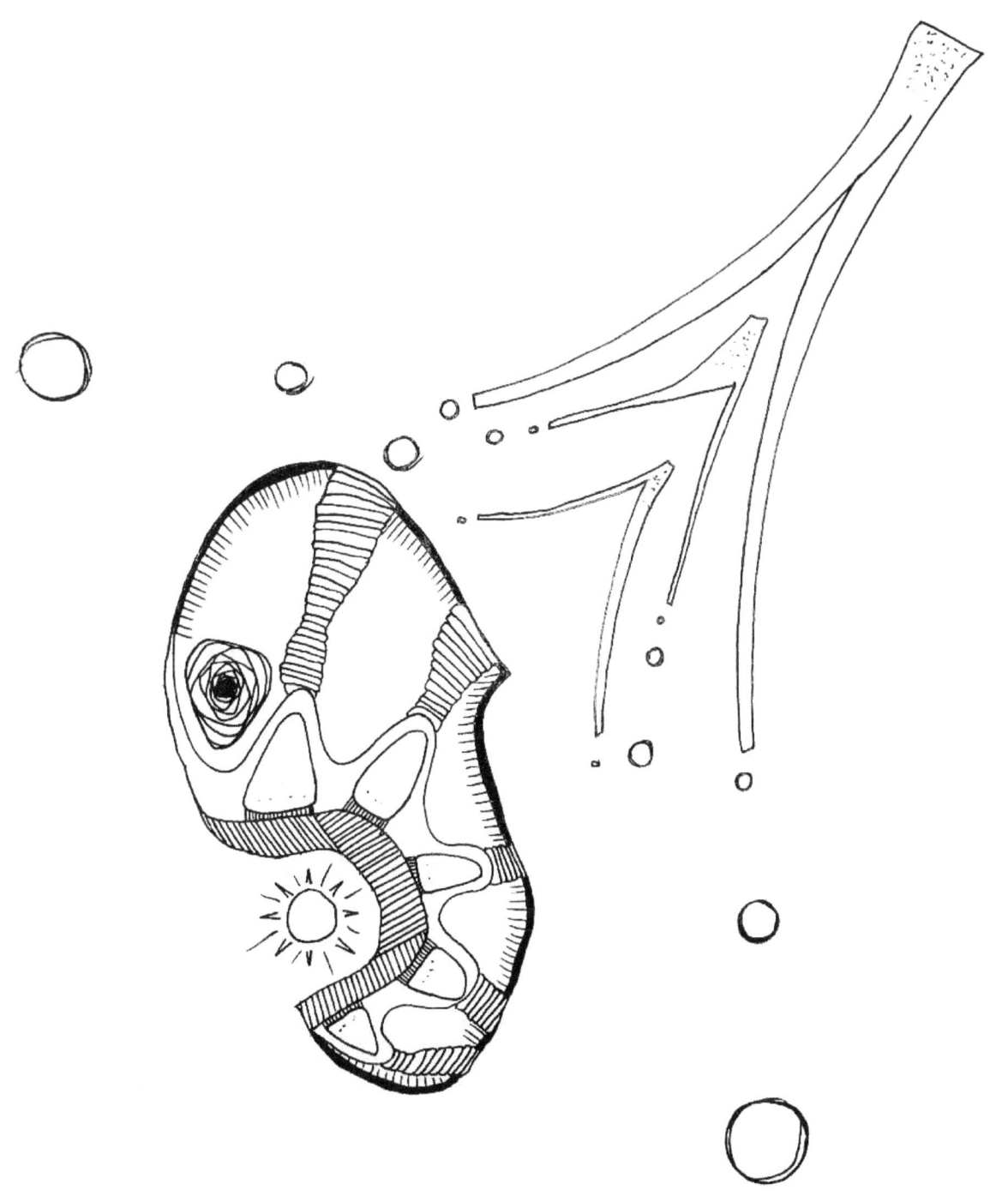

DEC 16
2020

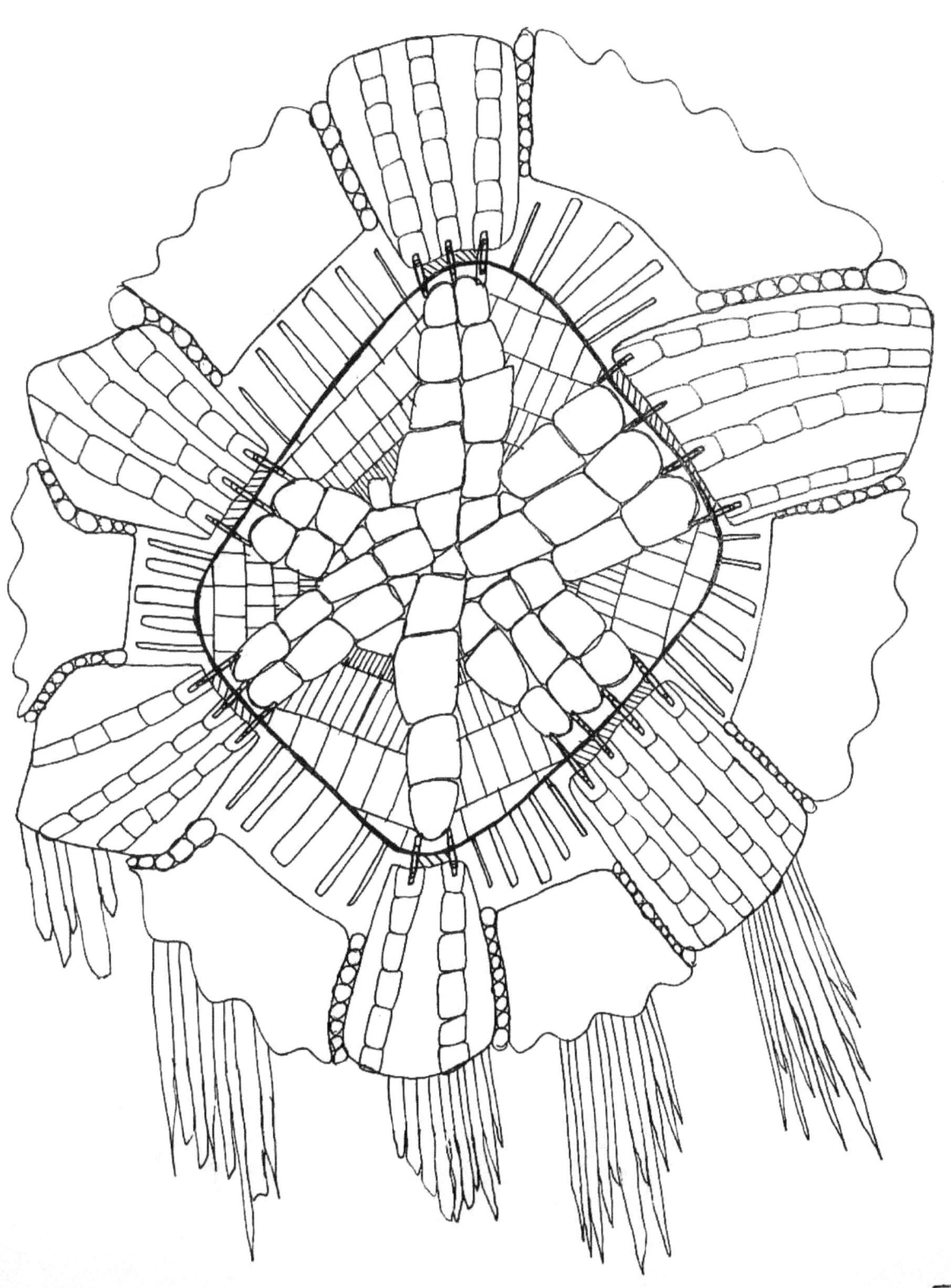

DEC 16

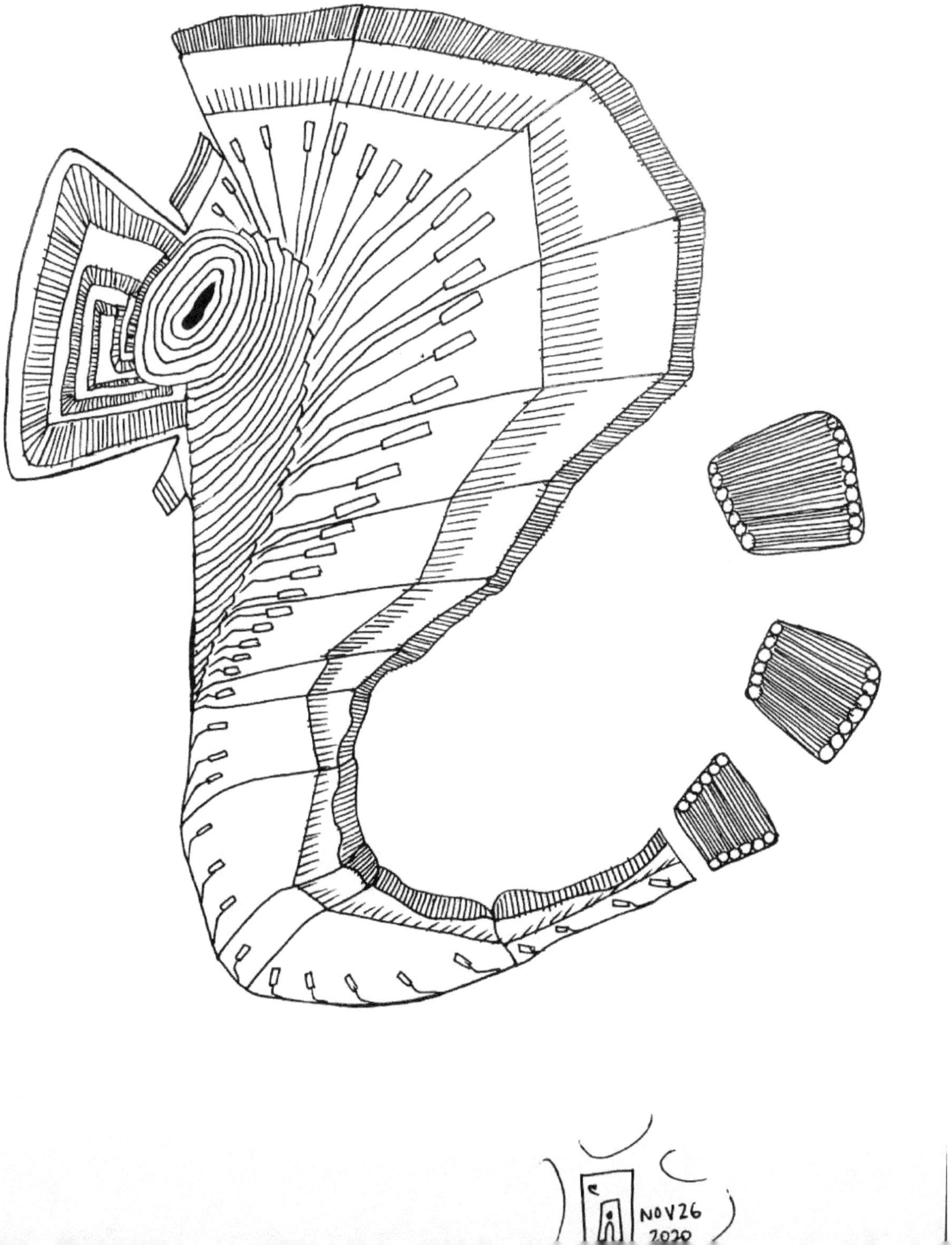

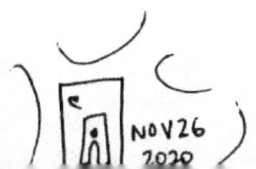

NOV 26
2020

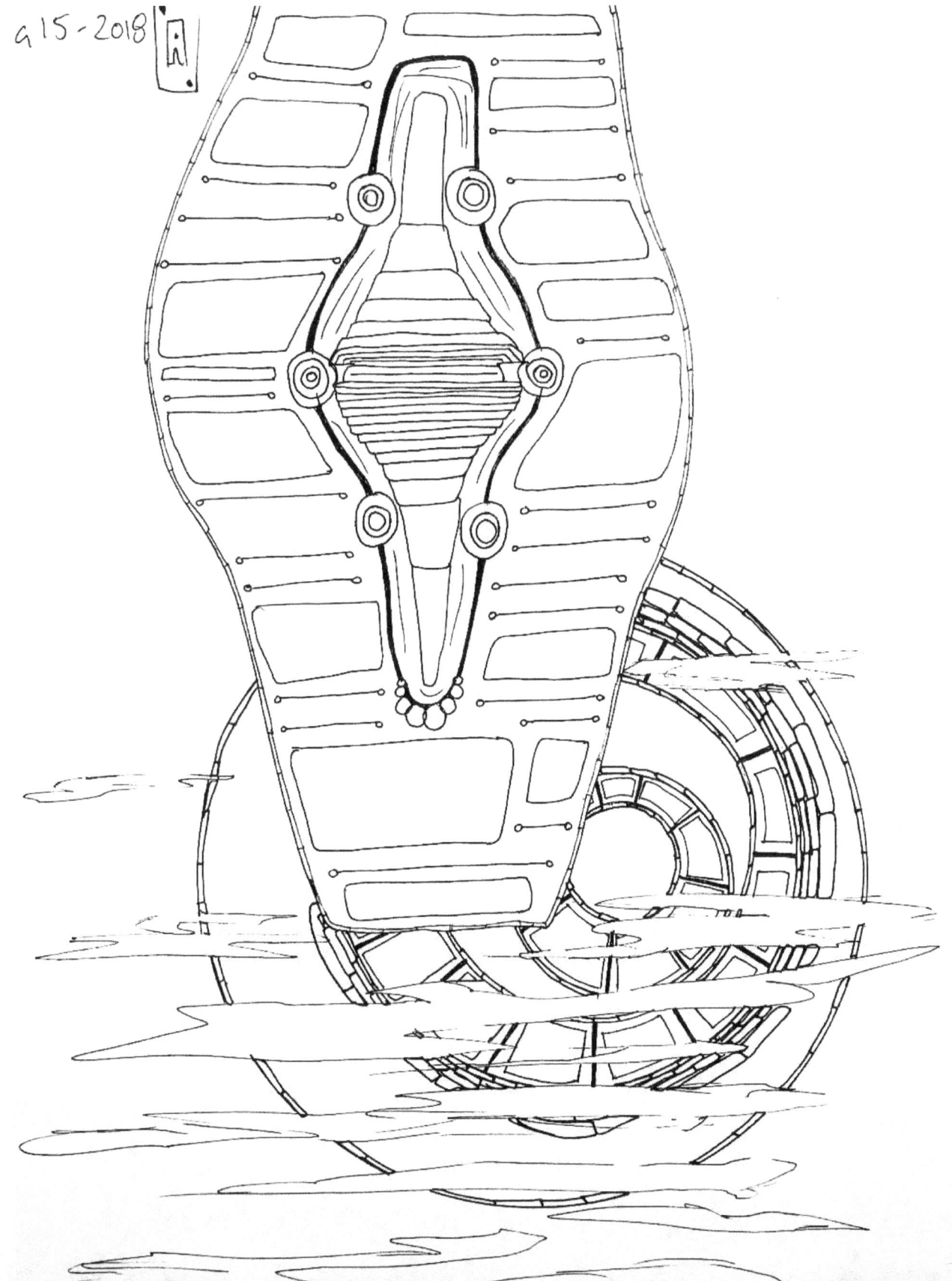

G15-2018

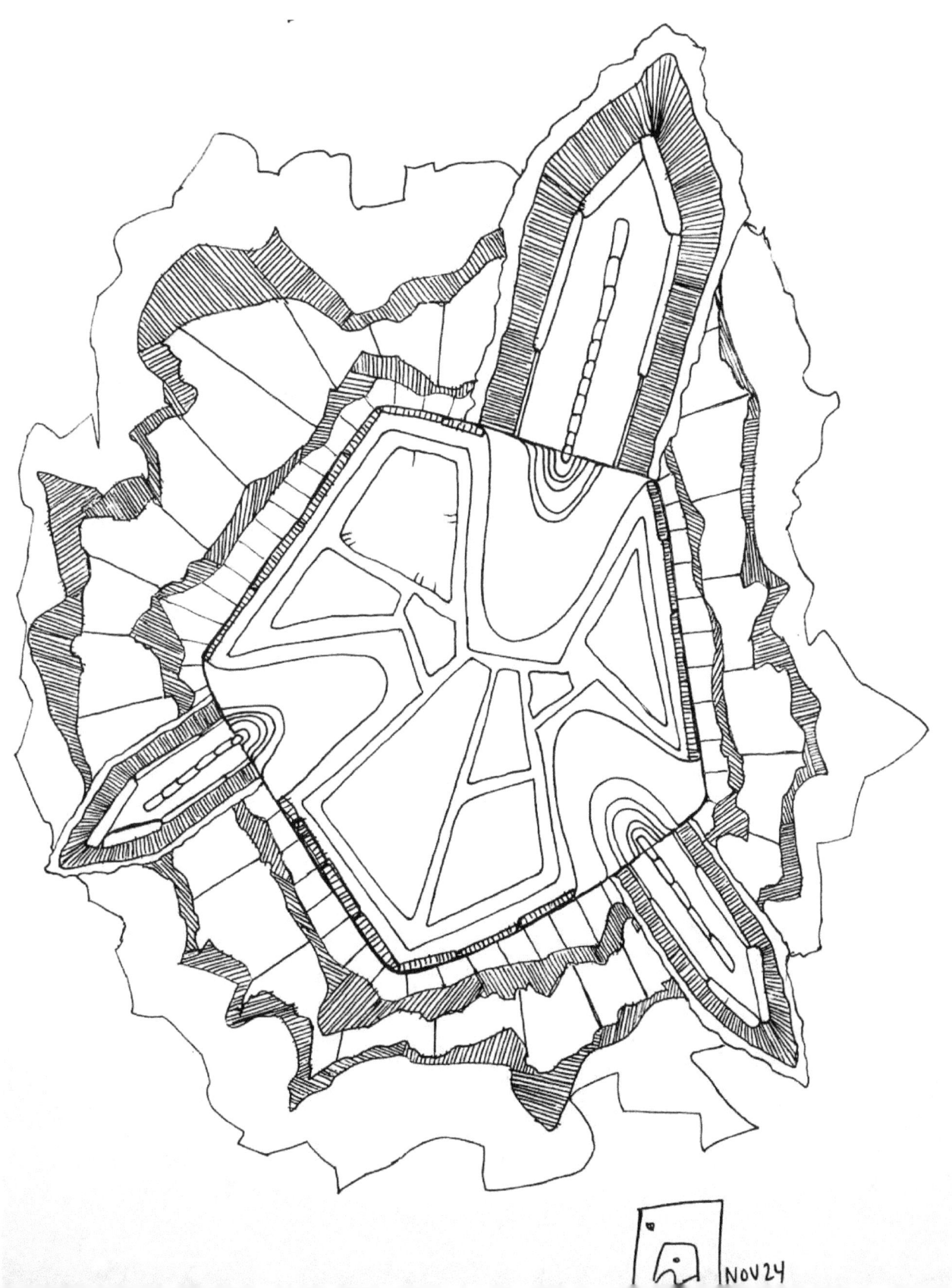

NOV24

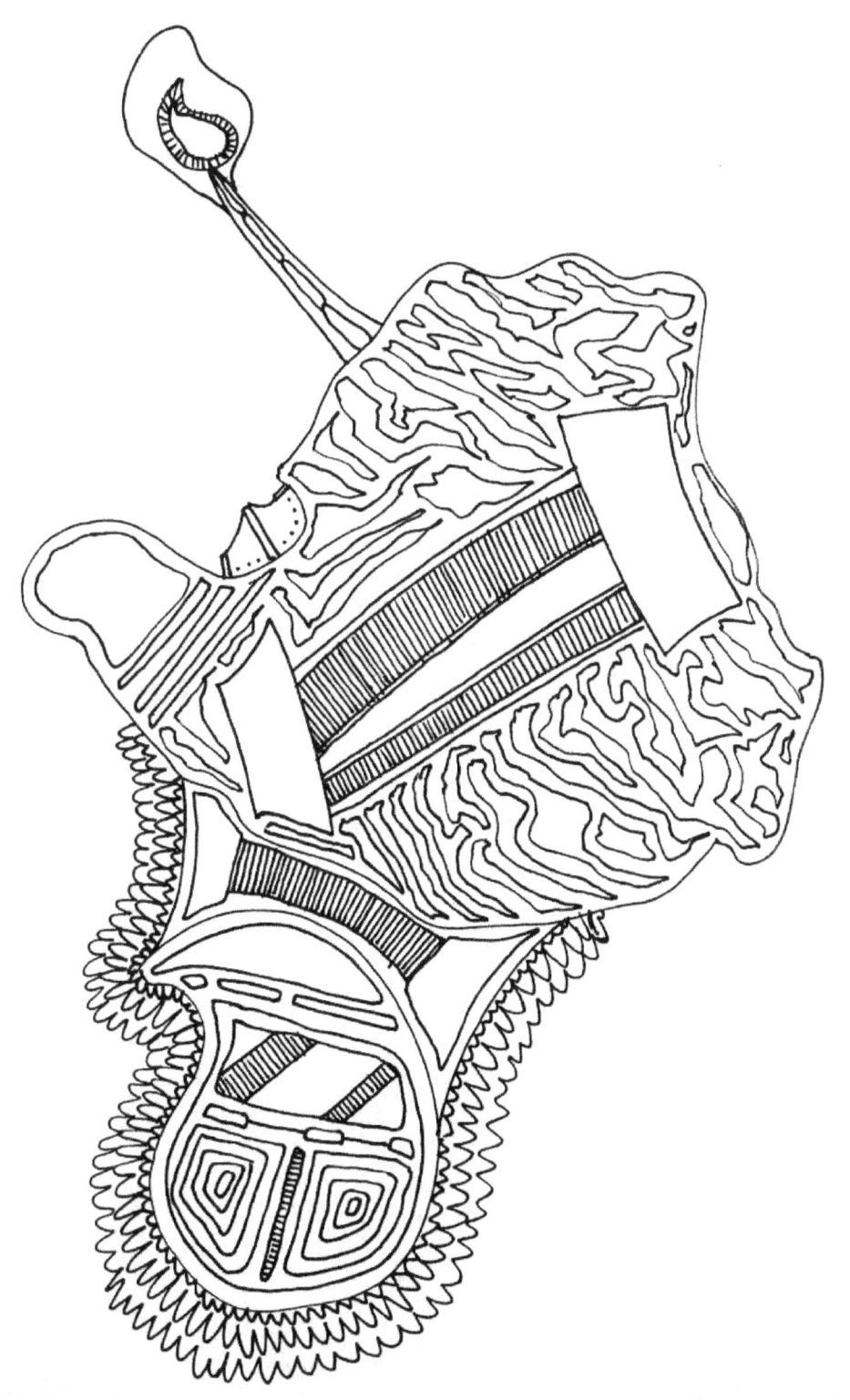

JAN 25
2021

CEREBRAL

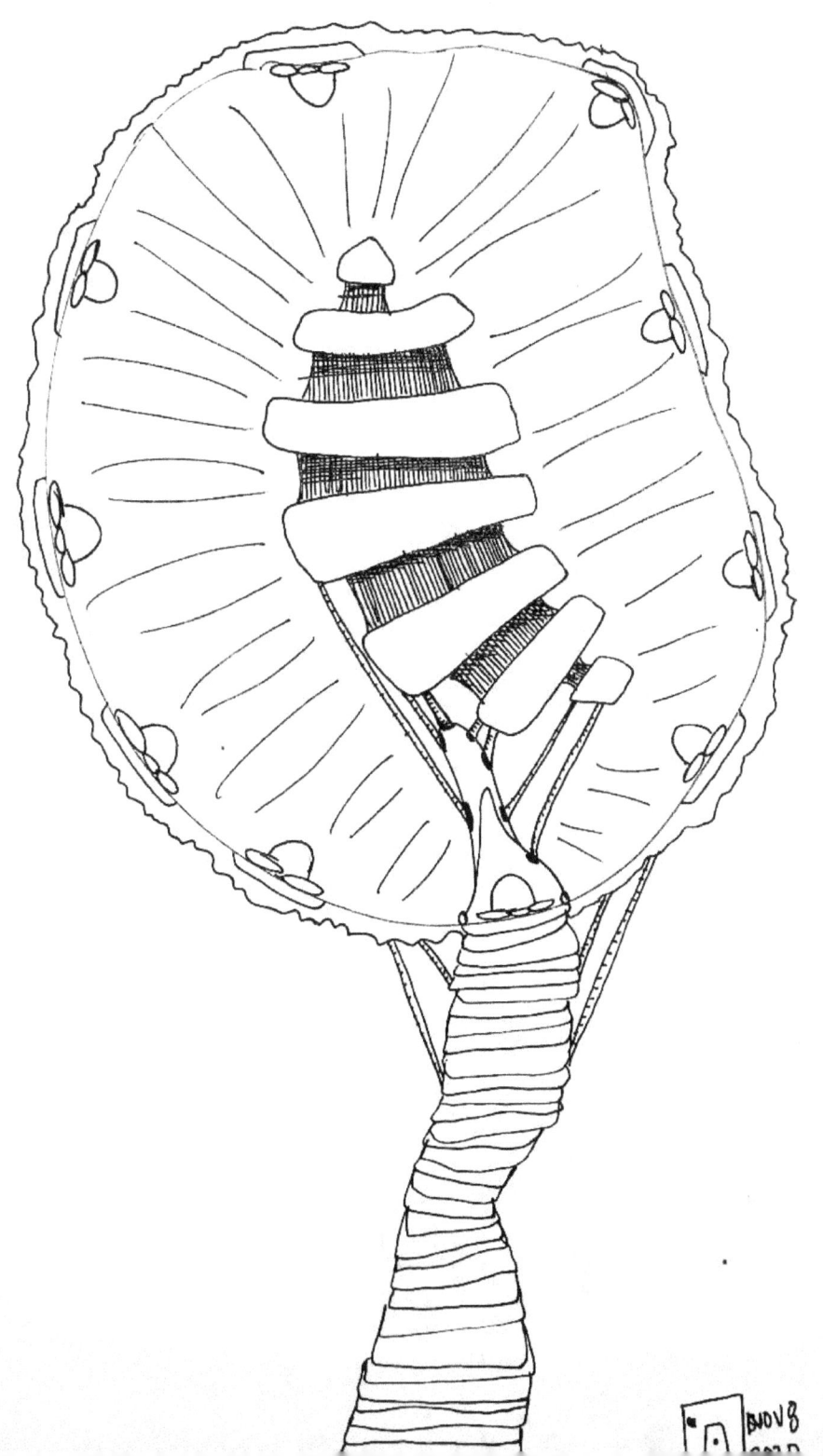

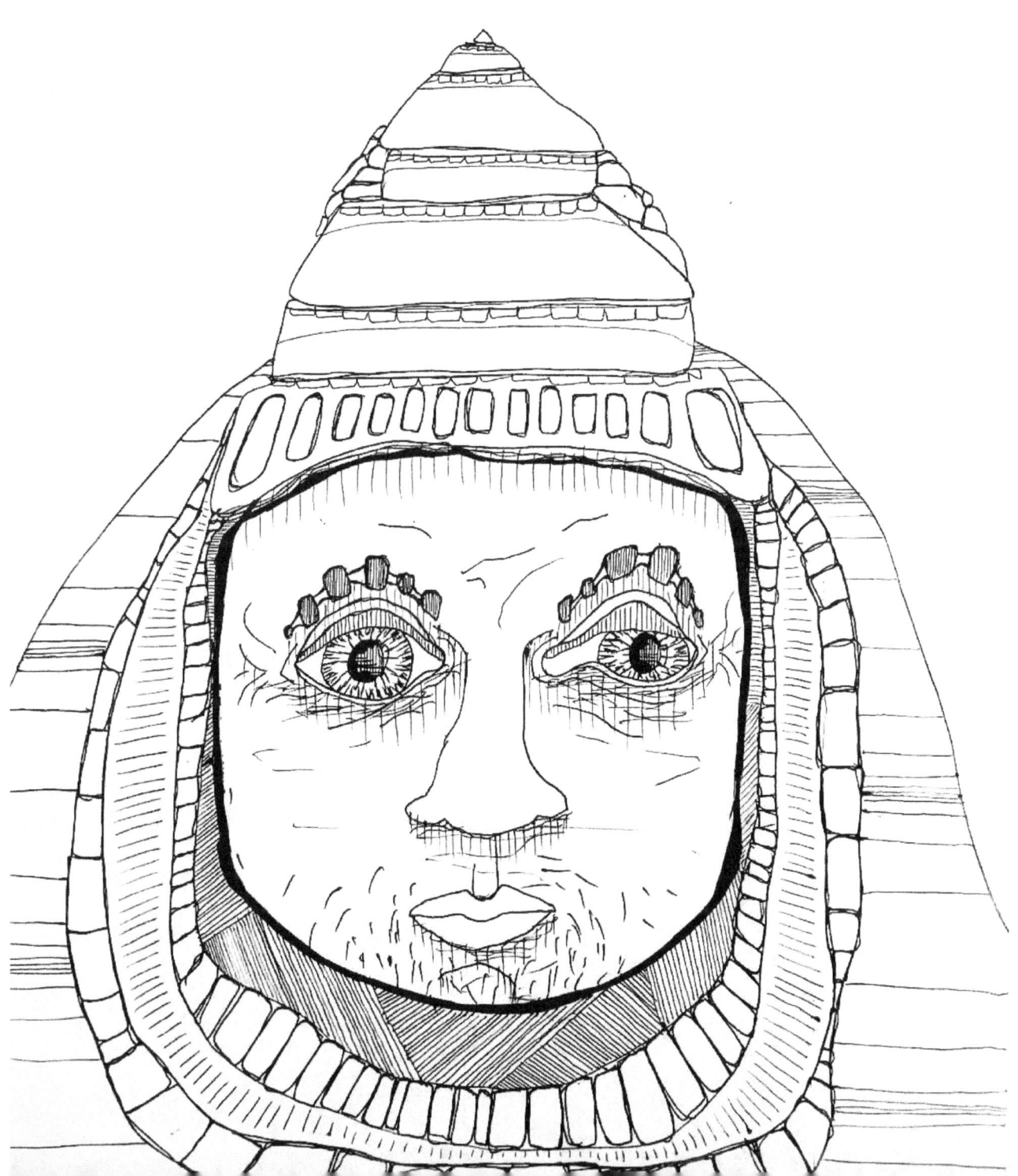

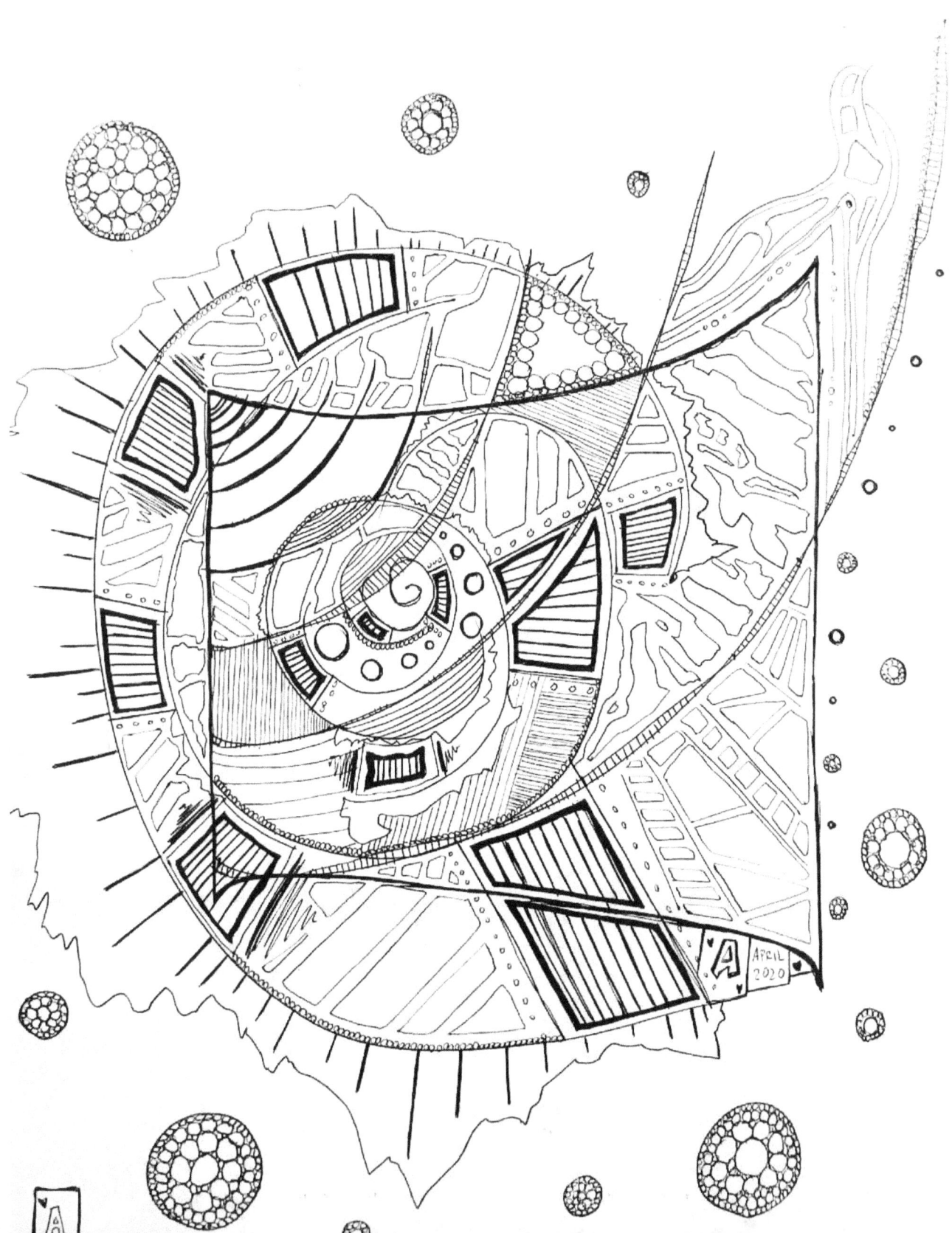

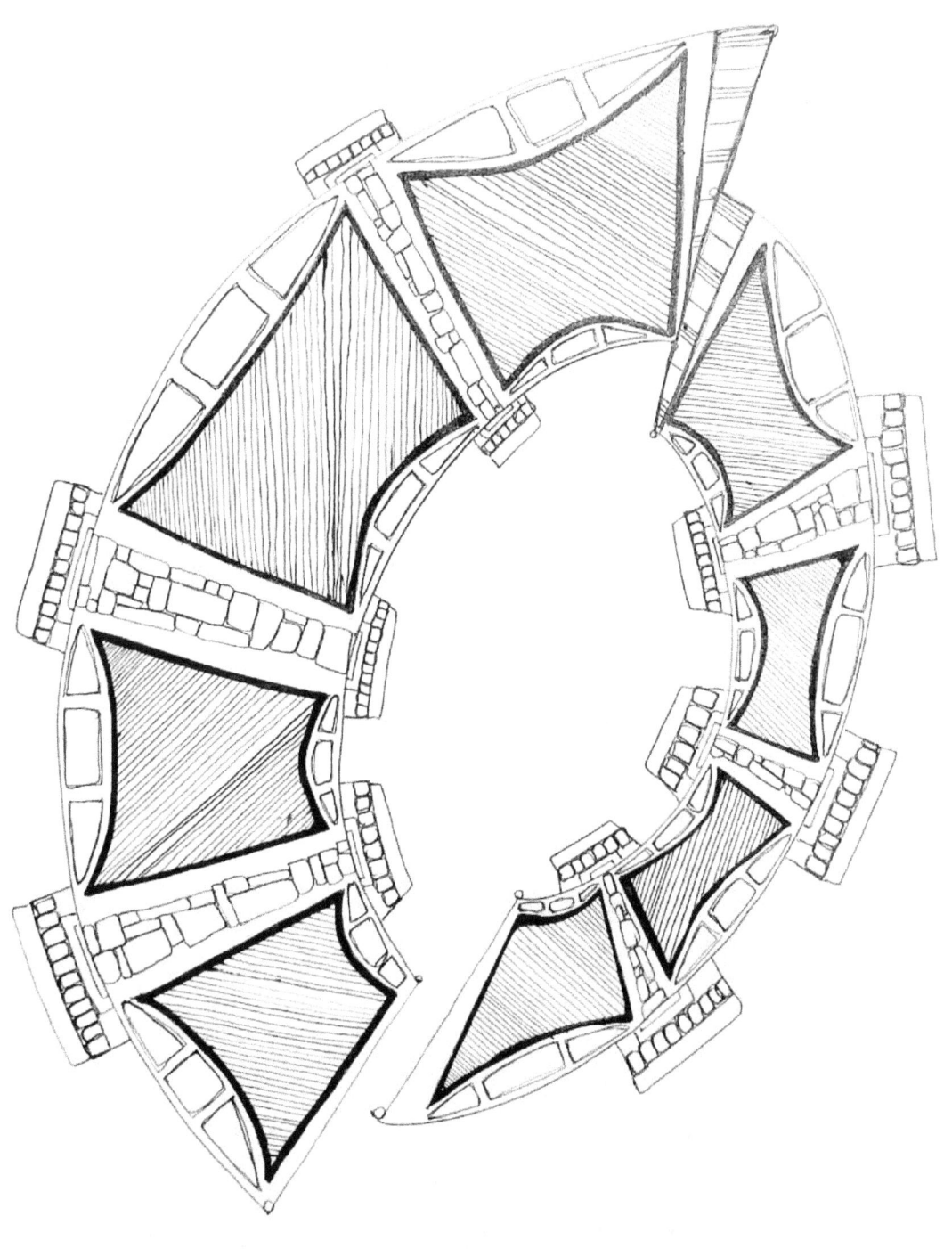

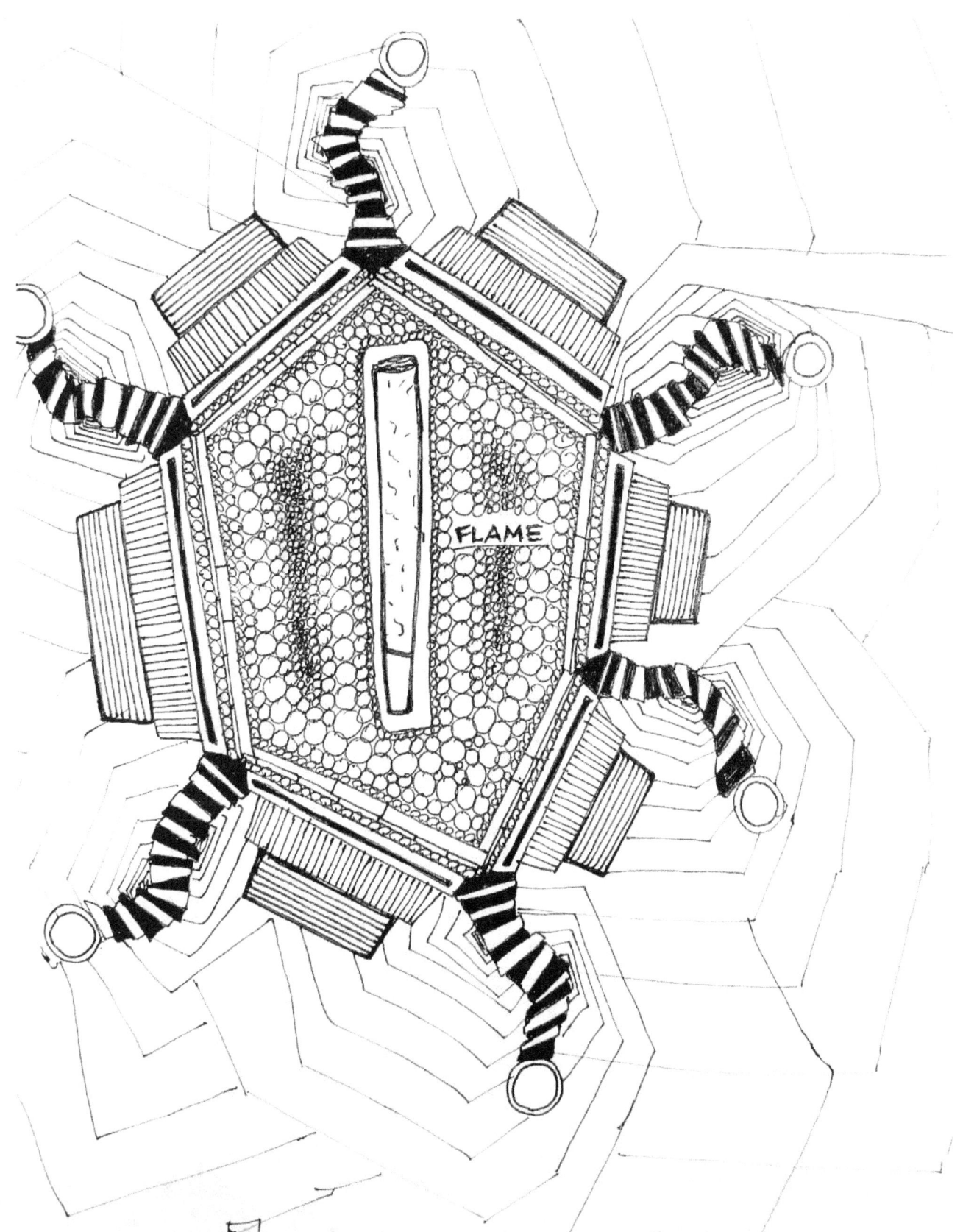

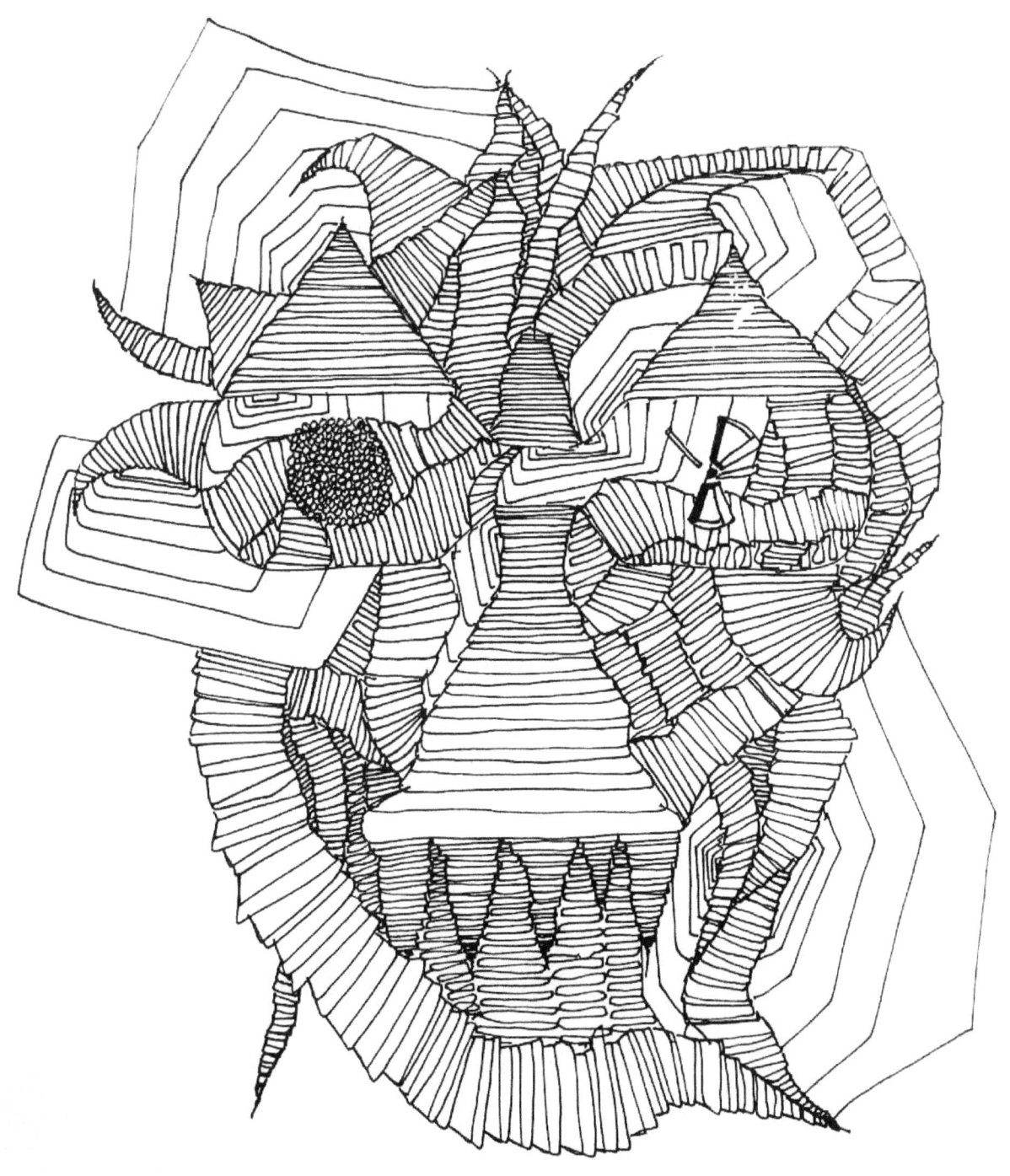

MARCH 13-2019

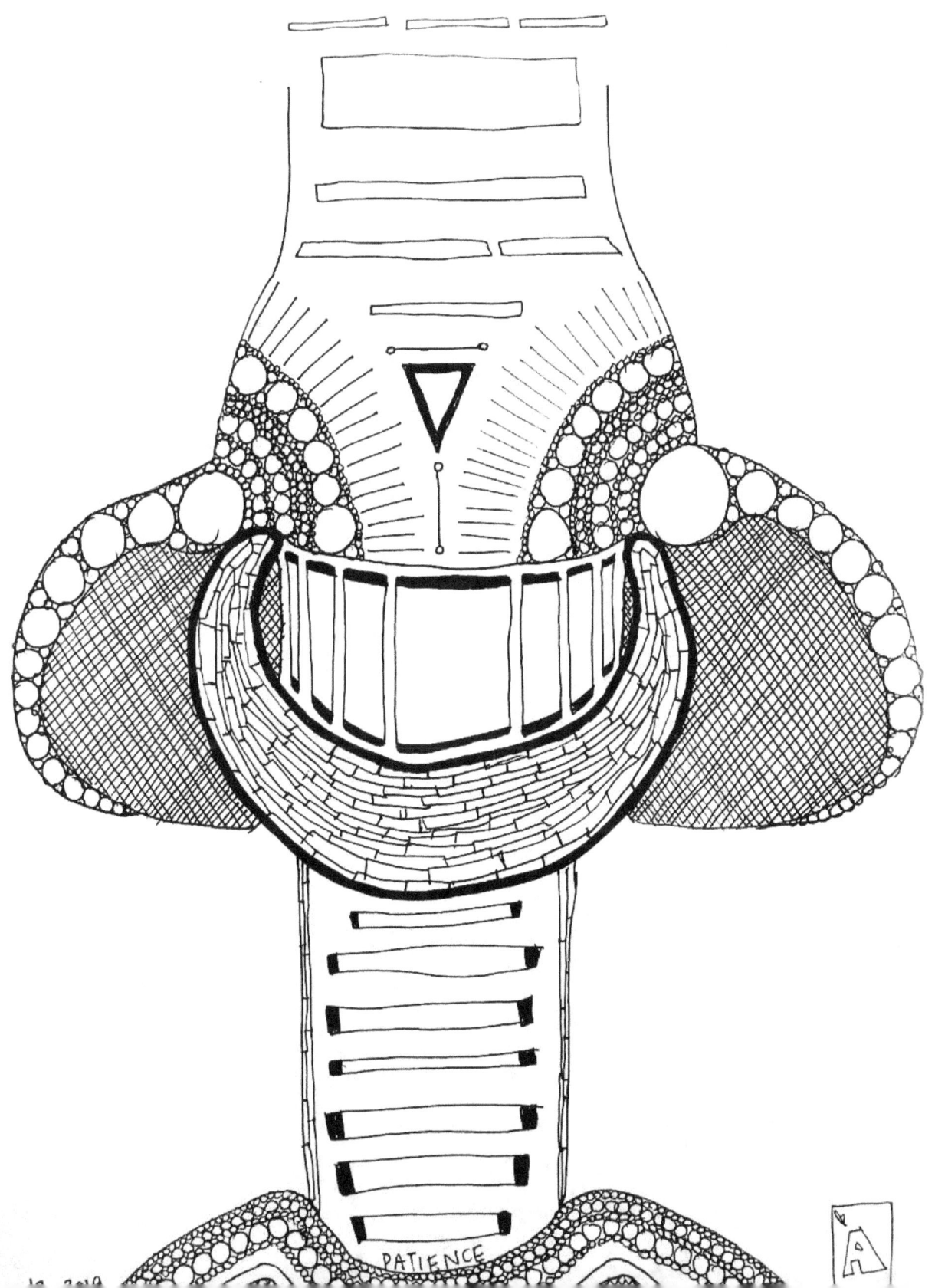

PATIENCE

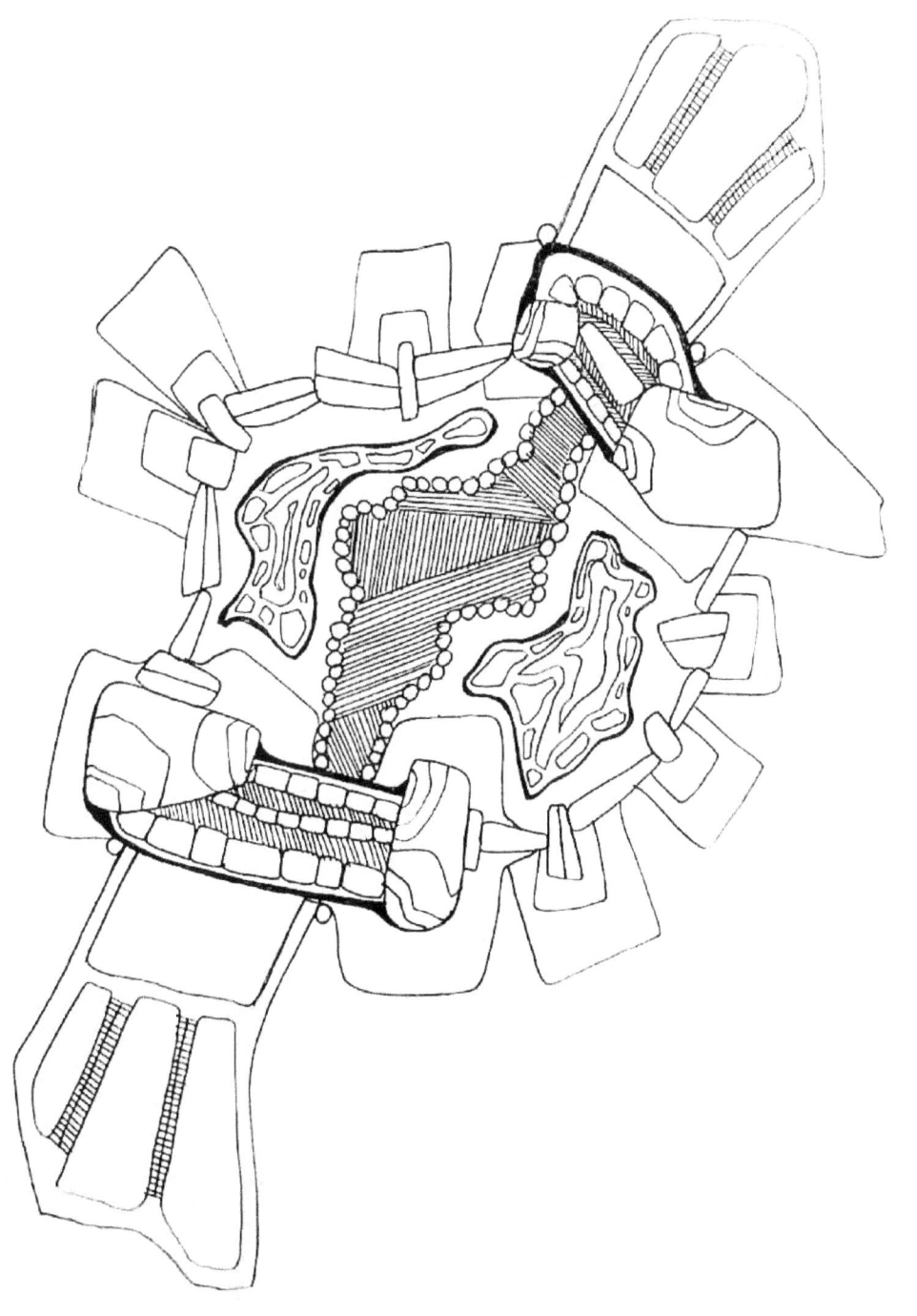

JANÓ
2021

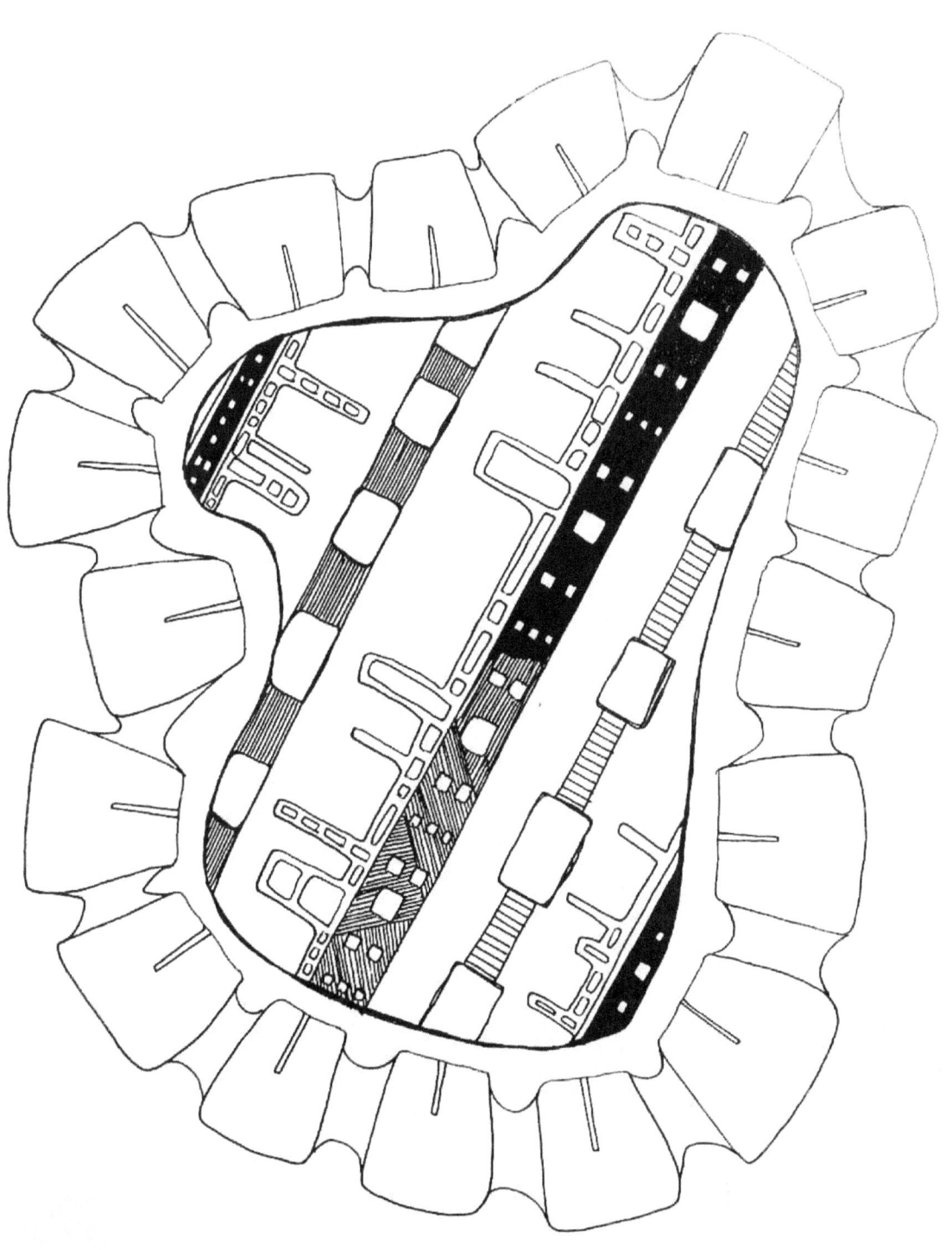

DEC 29
2020

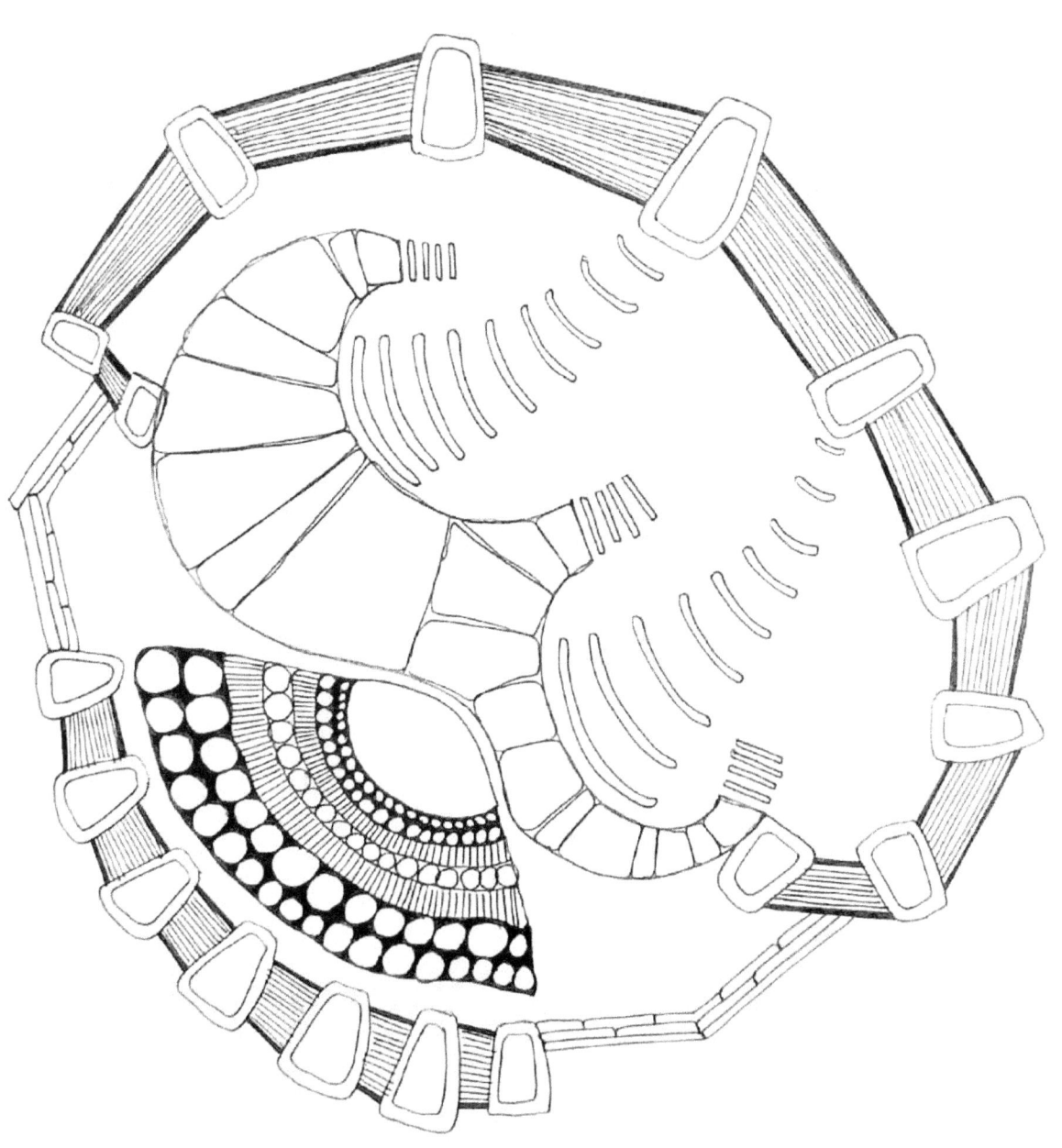

DEC17
2020

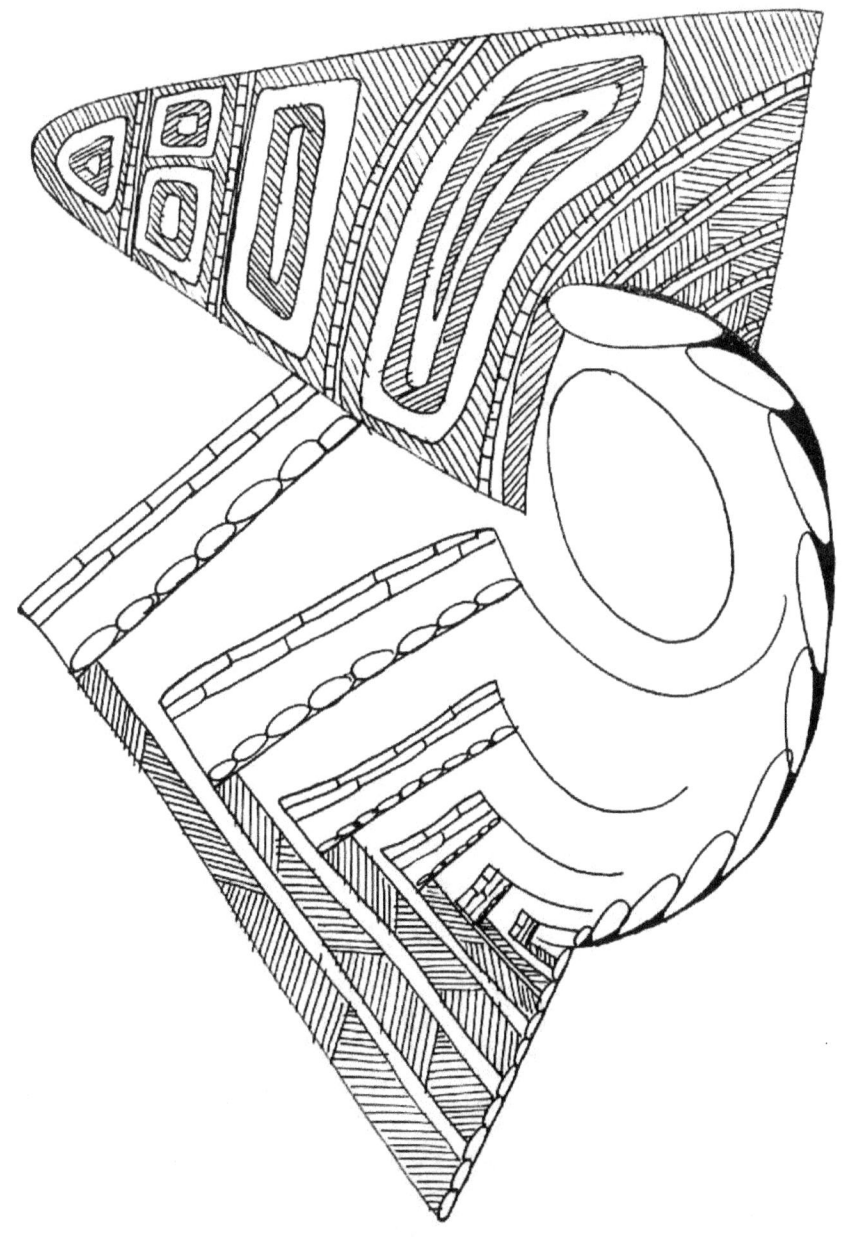

DEC 17
2020

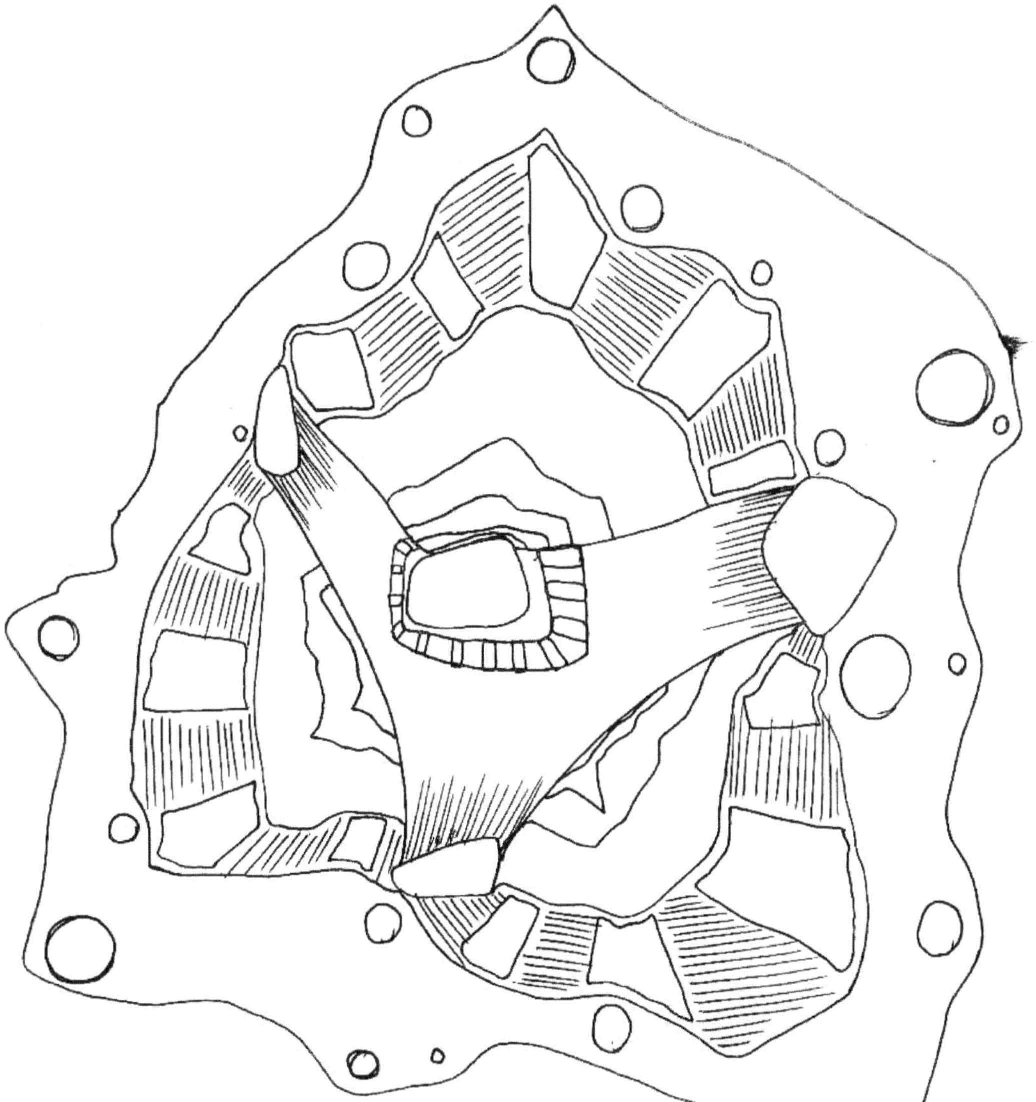

DEC 17
2020

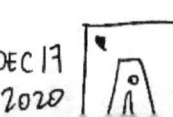

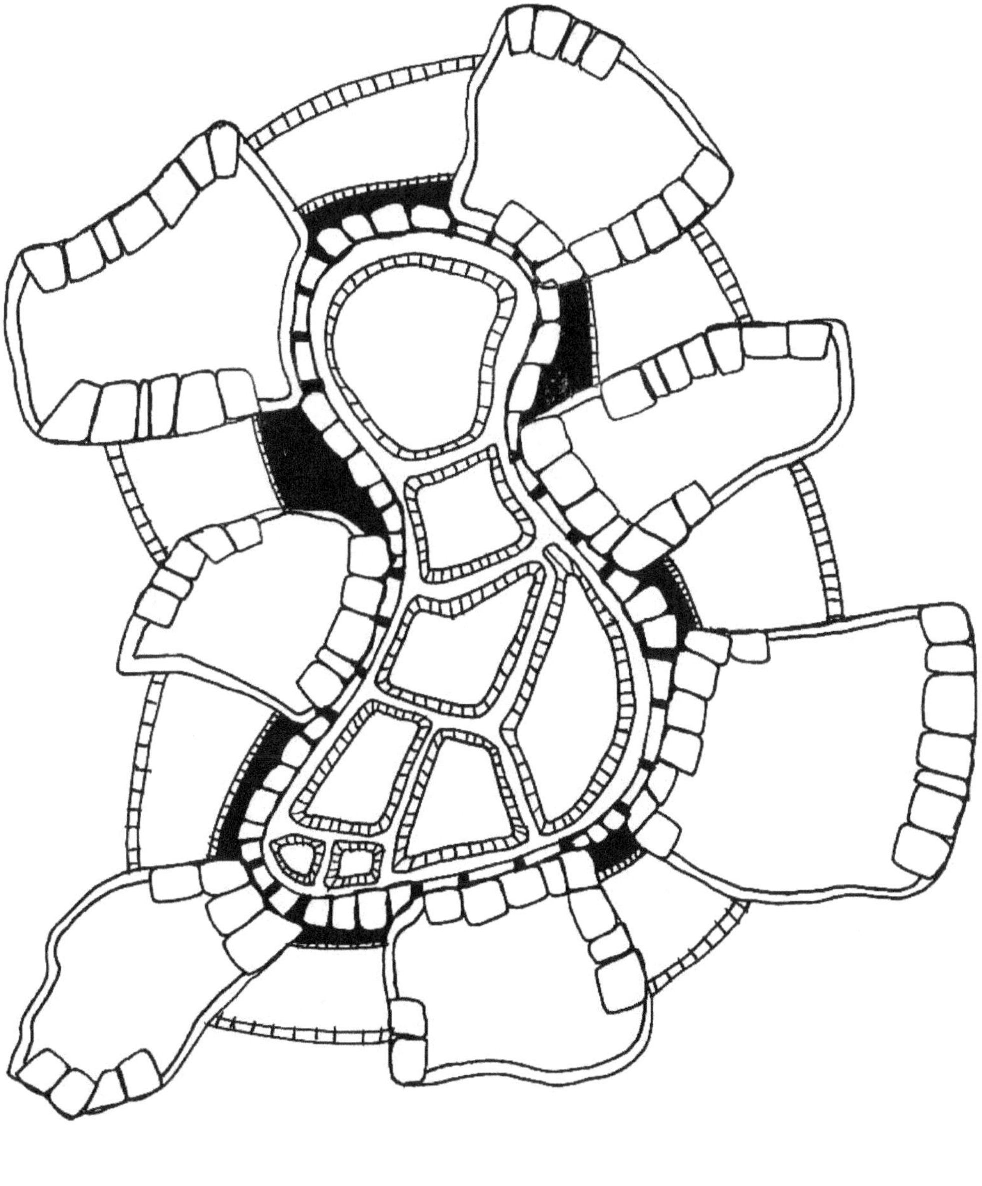

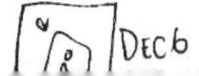
Dec 6

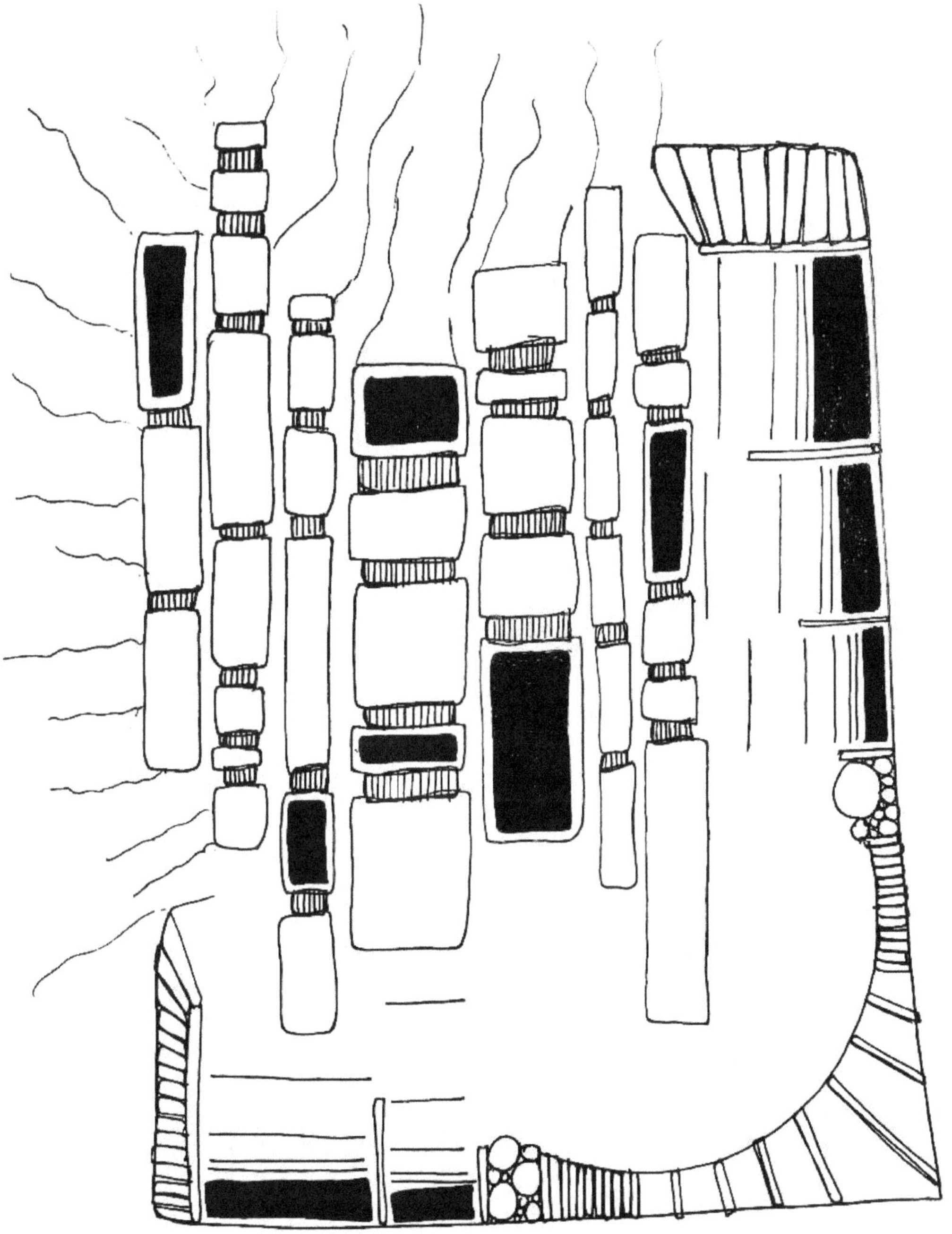

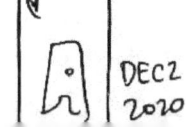

DEC2
2020

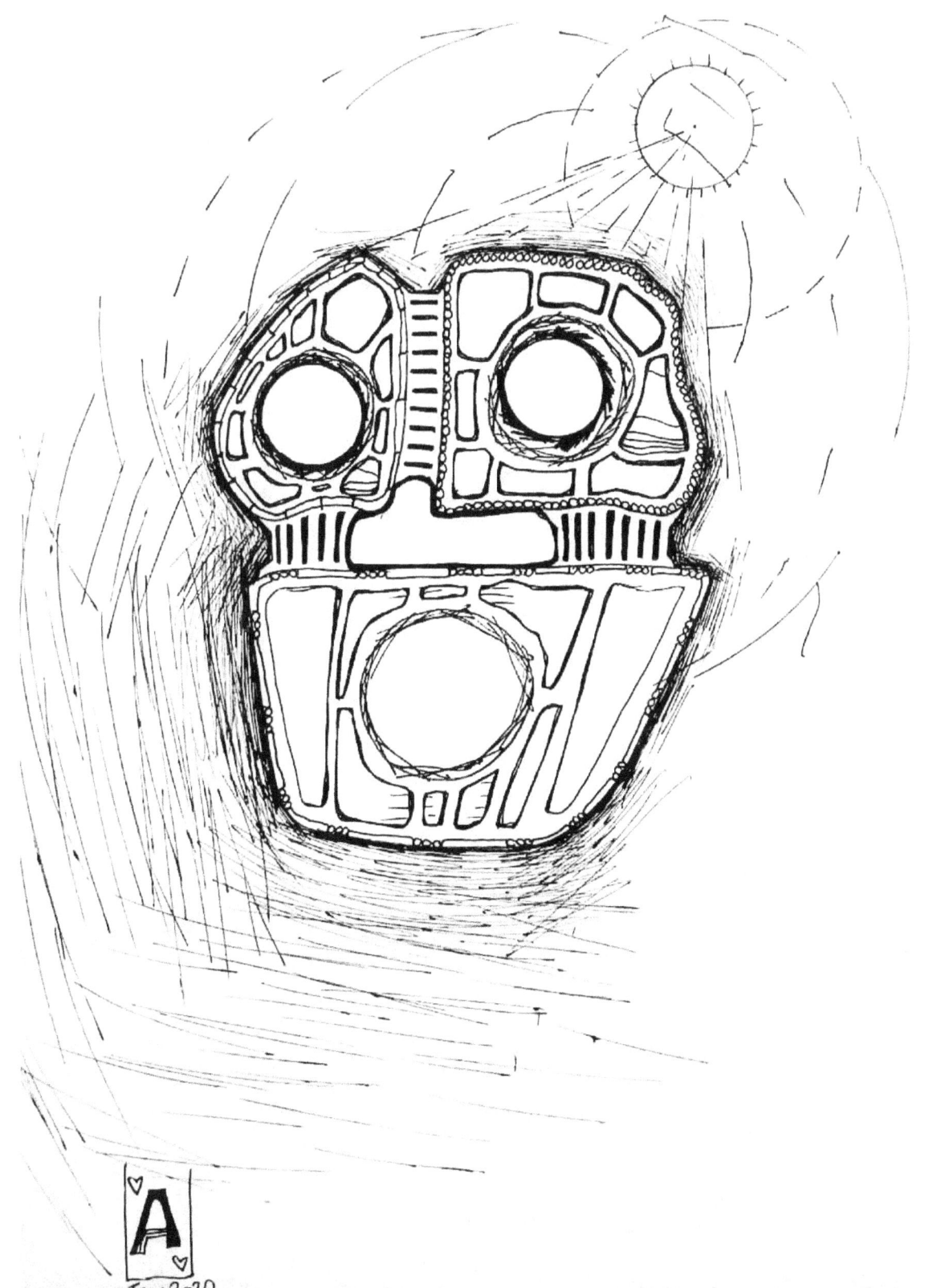

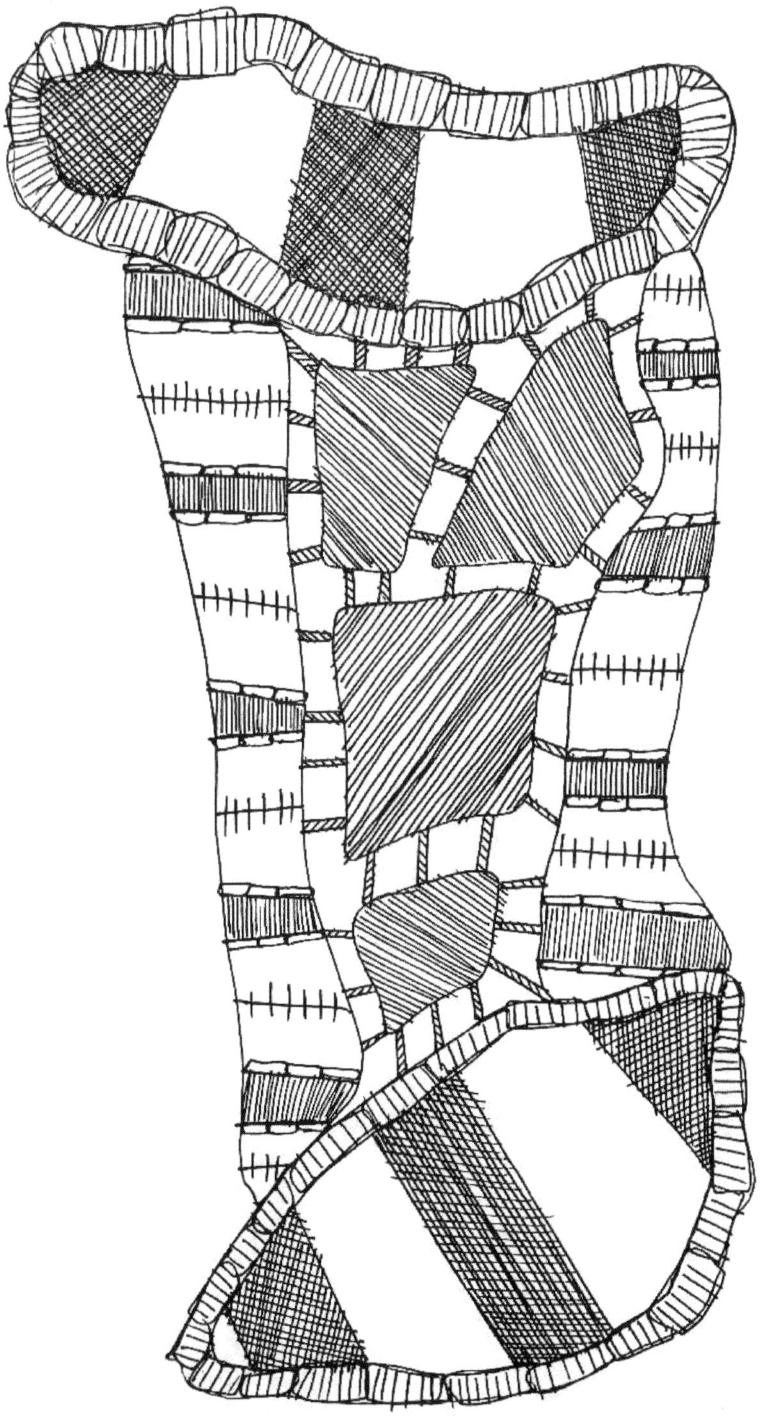

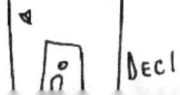

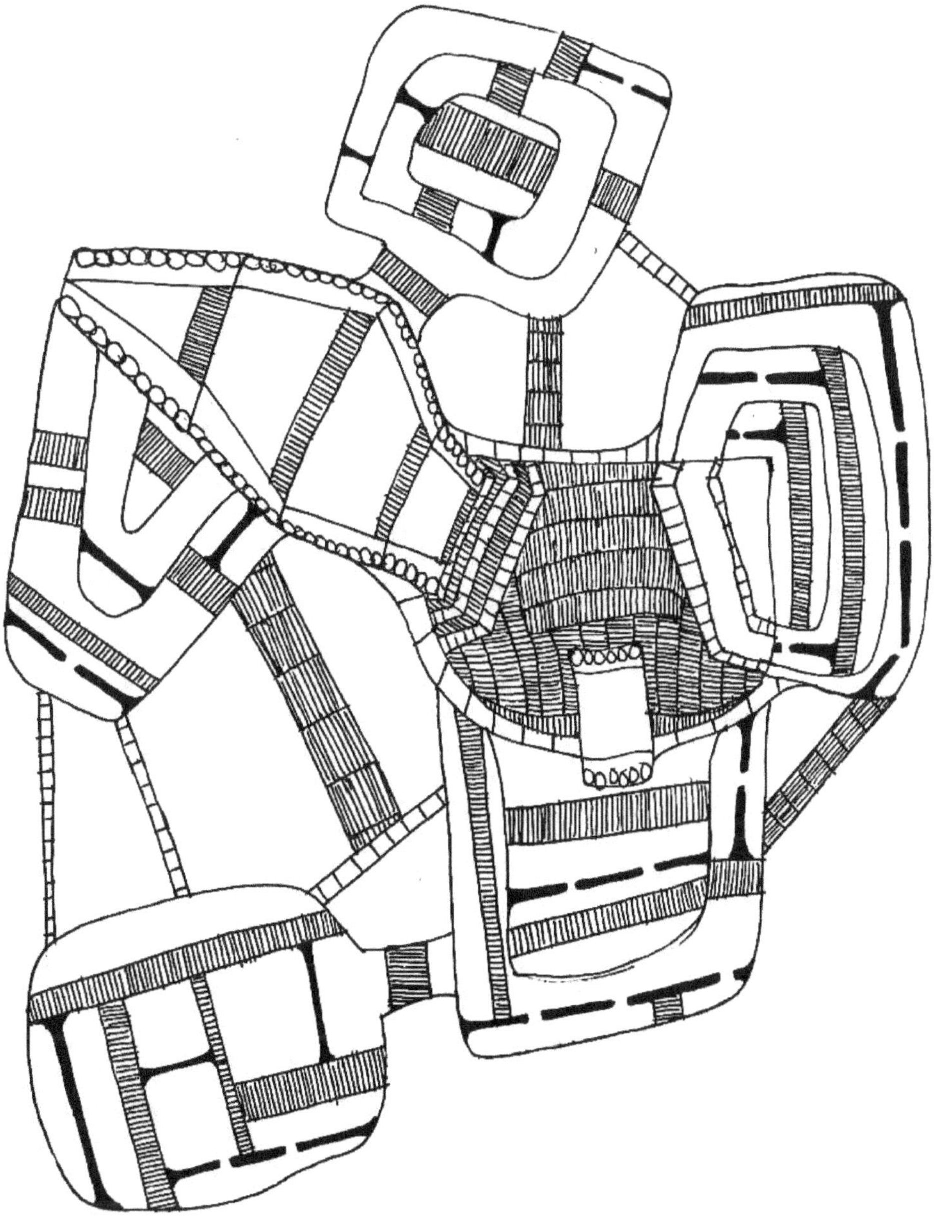

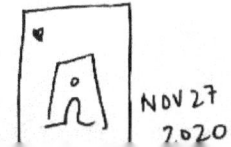

NOV 27
2020

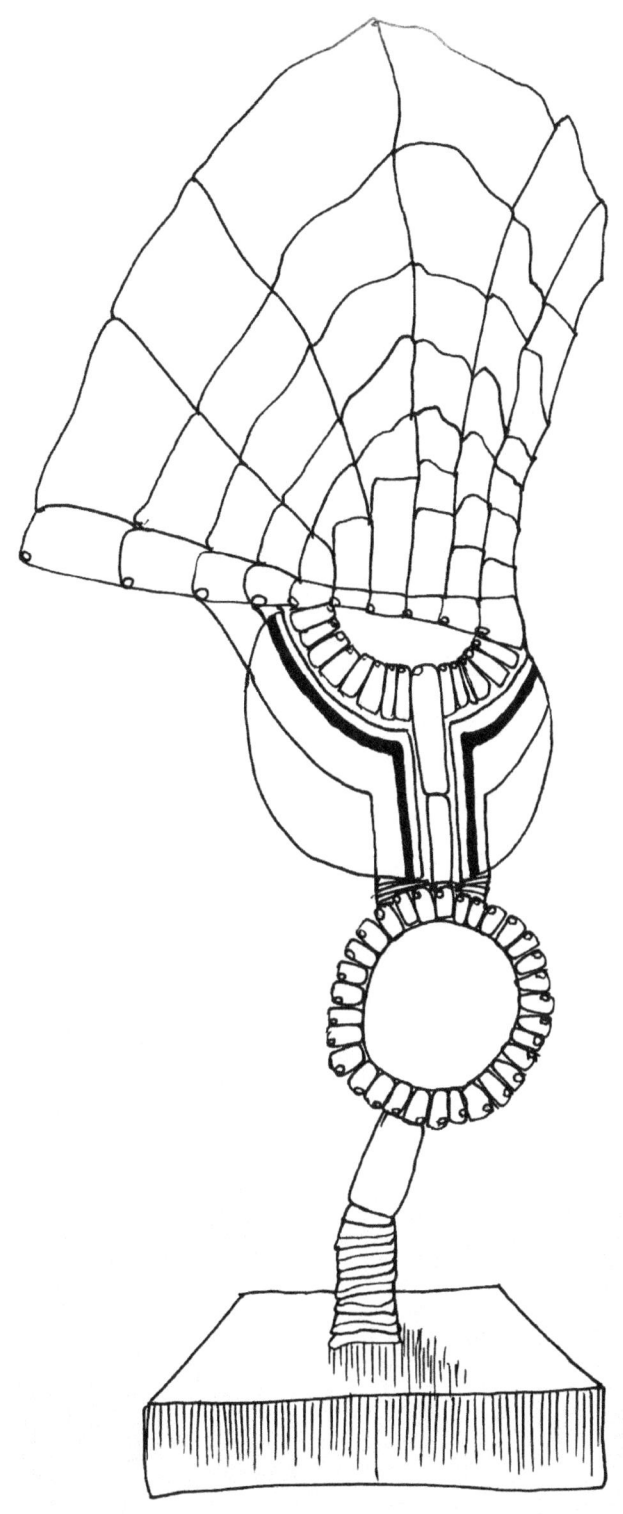

GRASPING FOR SOMETHING "ORIGINAL"
SOMETHING THAT IS BEYOND ORDINARY
IS AN EXERCISE IN UNDERSTANDING REALITY.

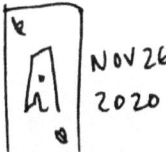

NOV 26
2020

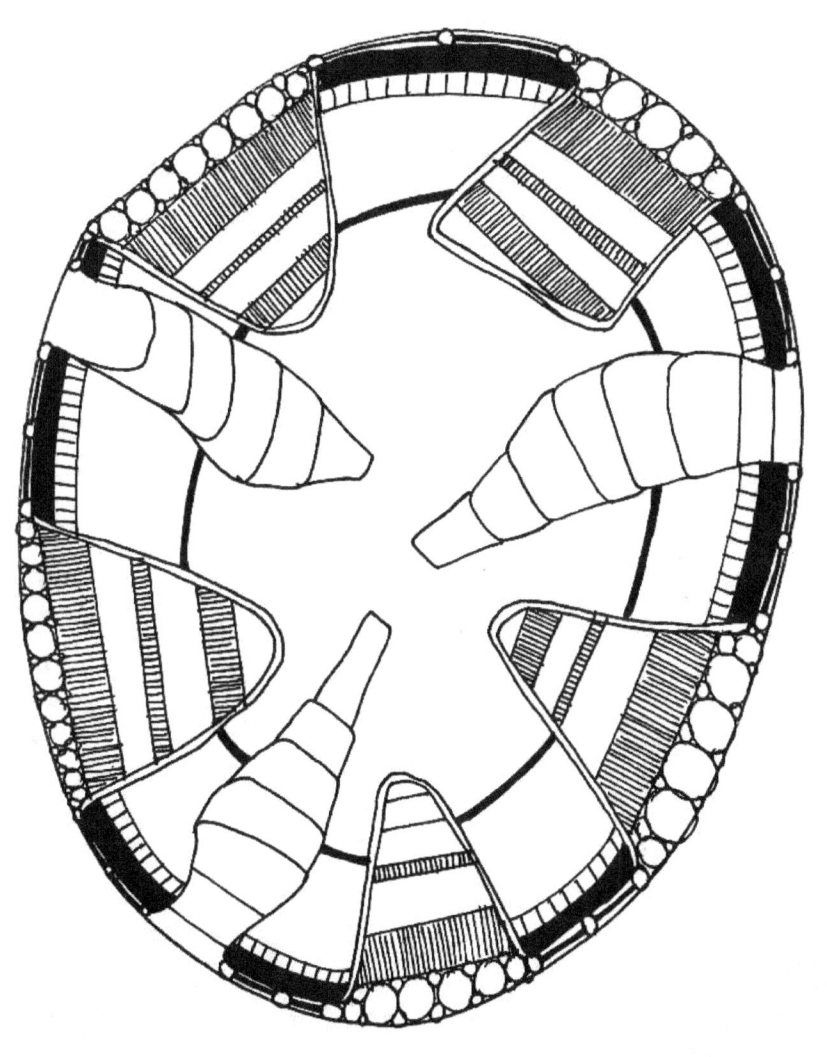

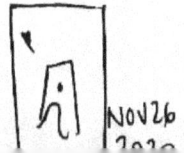
NOV 26
2020

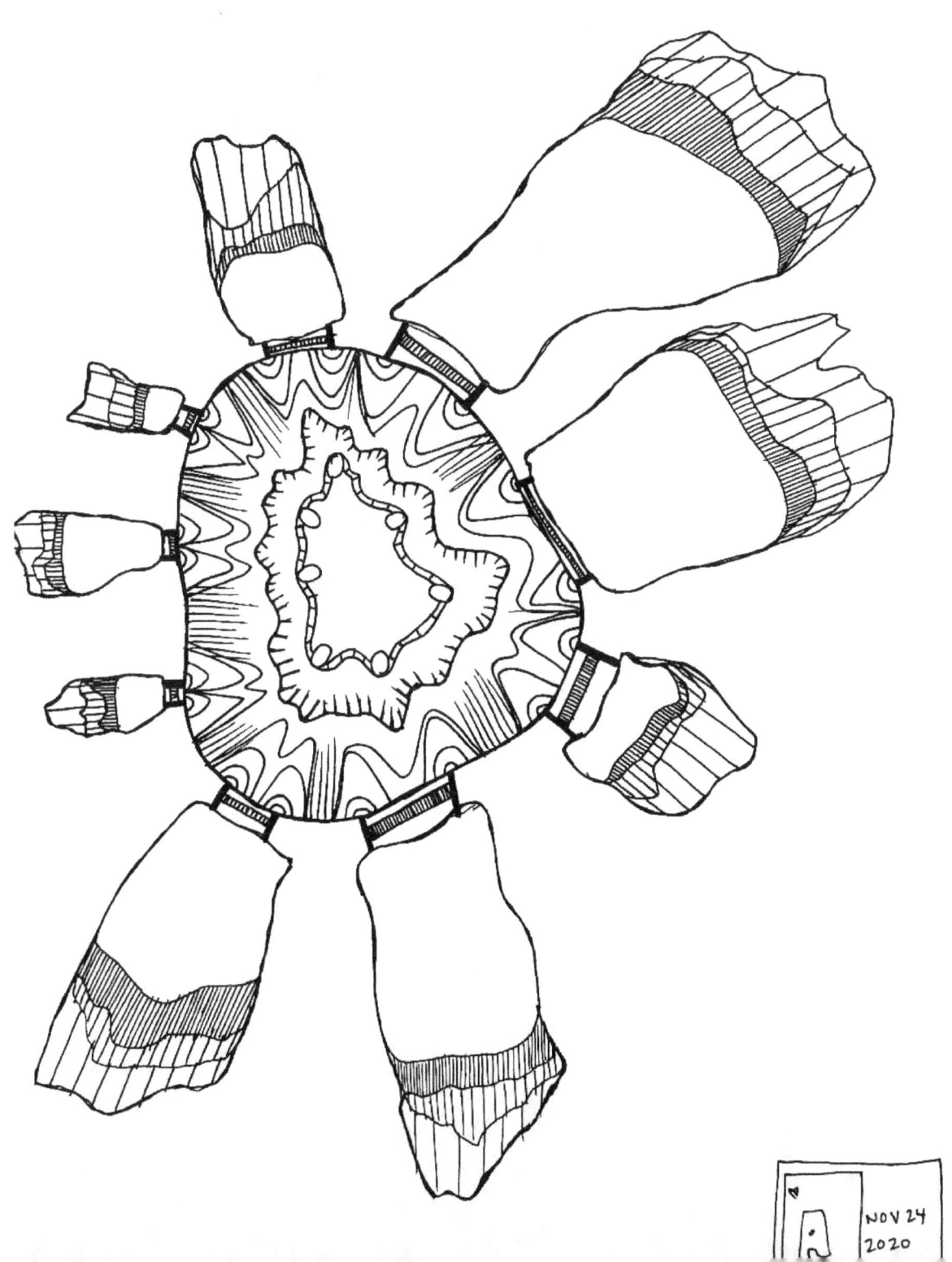

NOV 24
2020

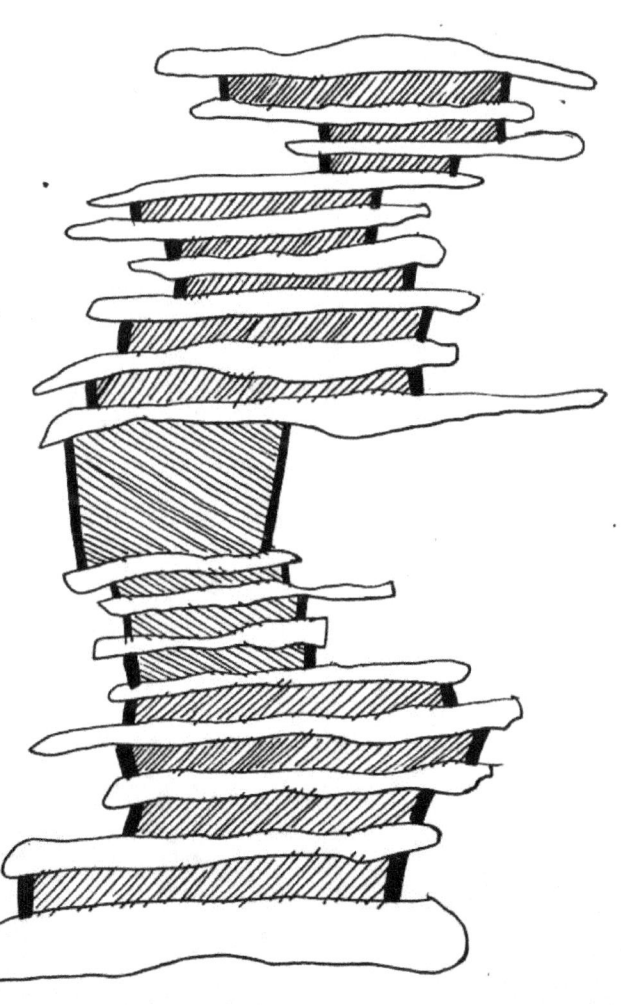

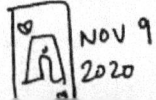 NOV 9
2020

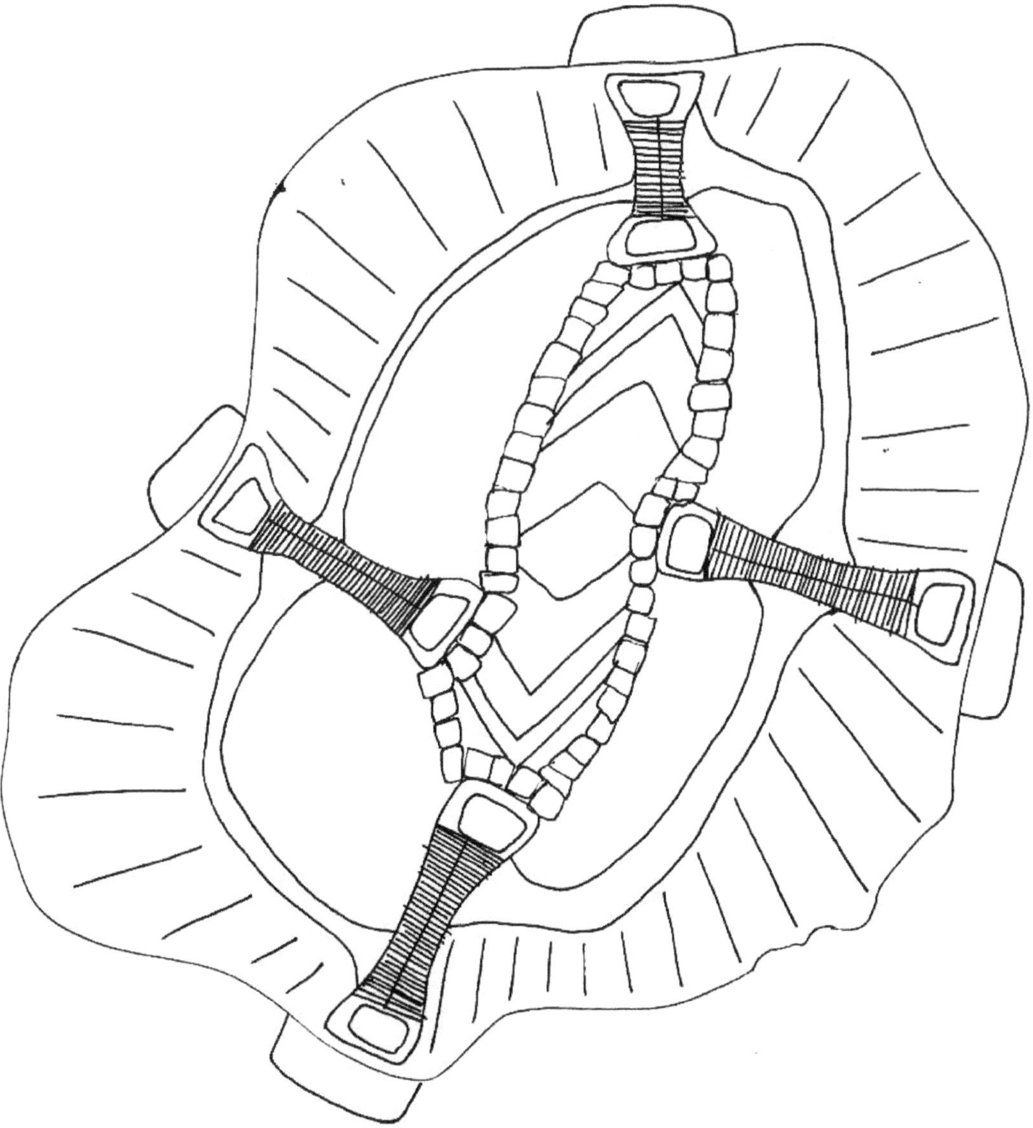

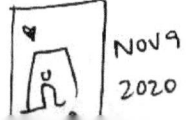

Nov 9
2020

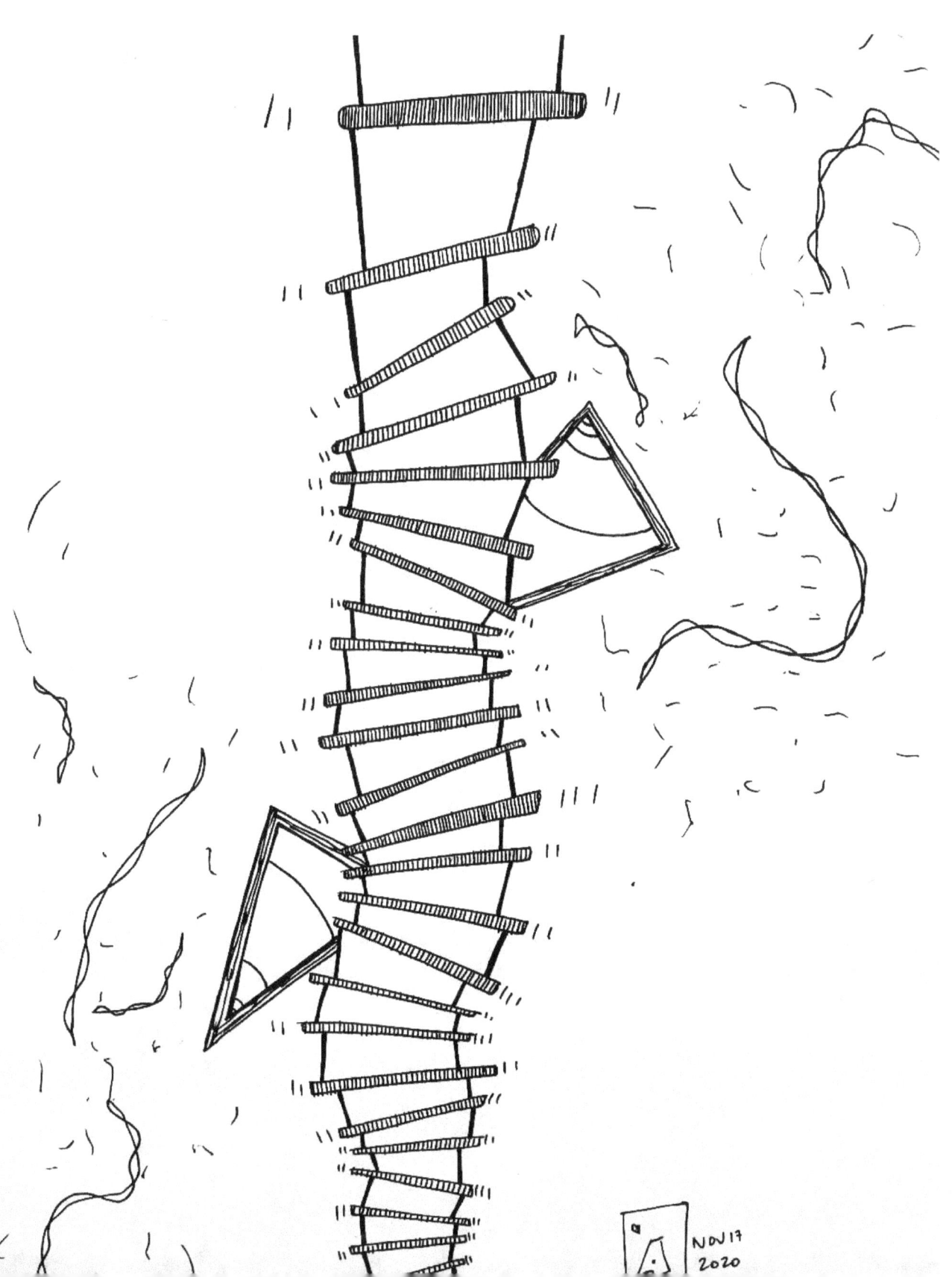

NOV 17
2020

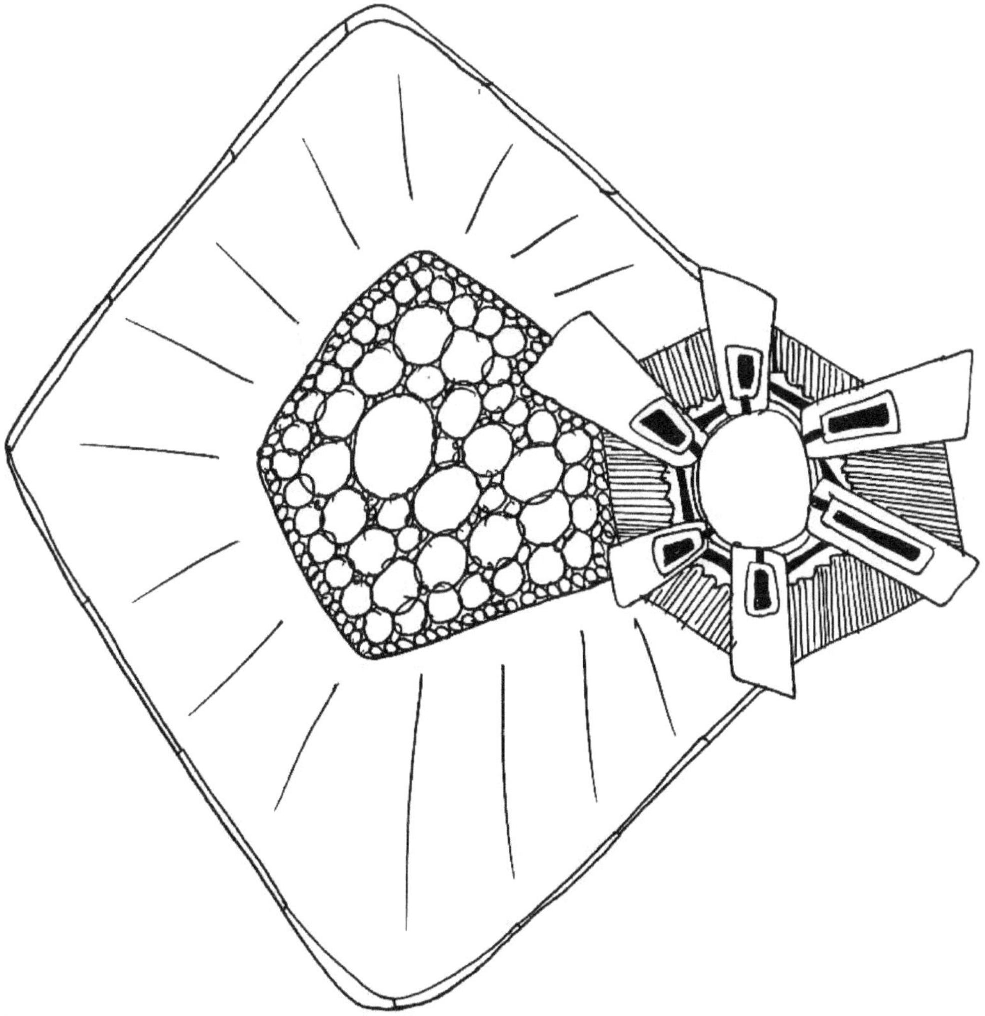

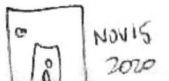

NOVIS
2020

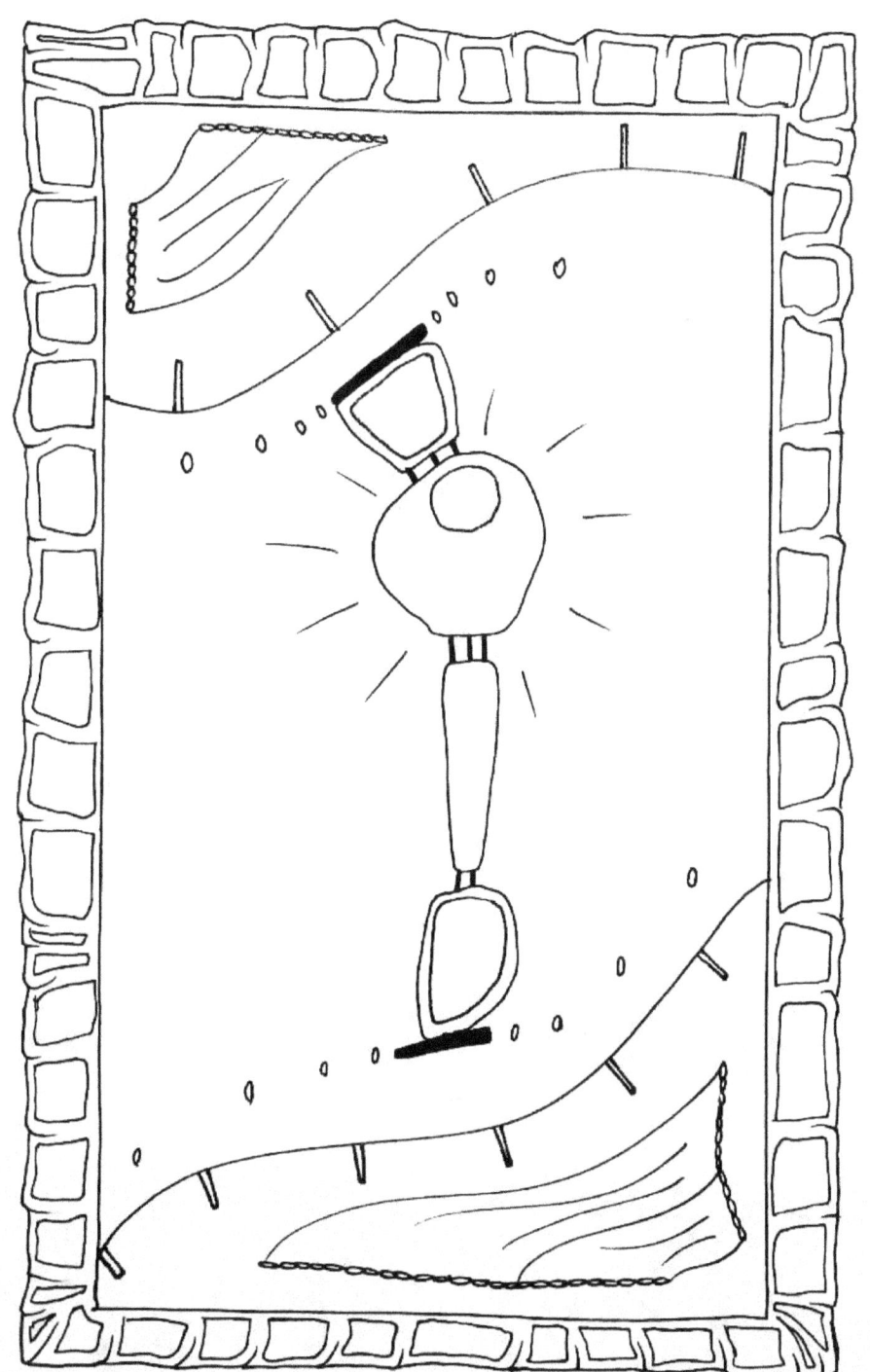

JAN 25
2021

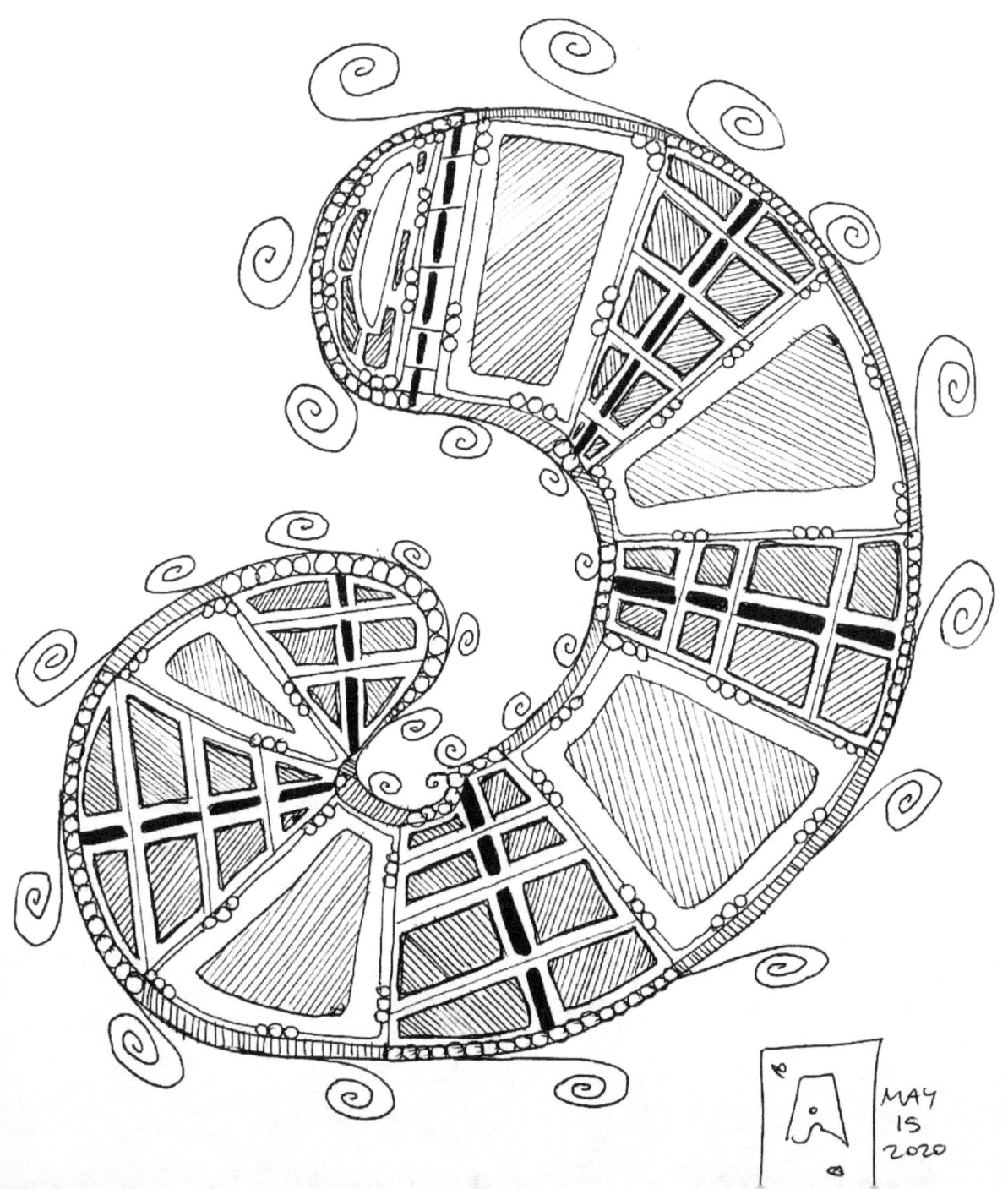

MAY
15
2020

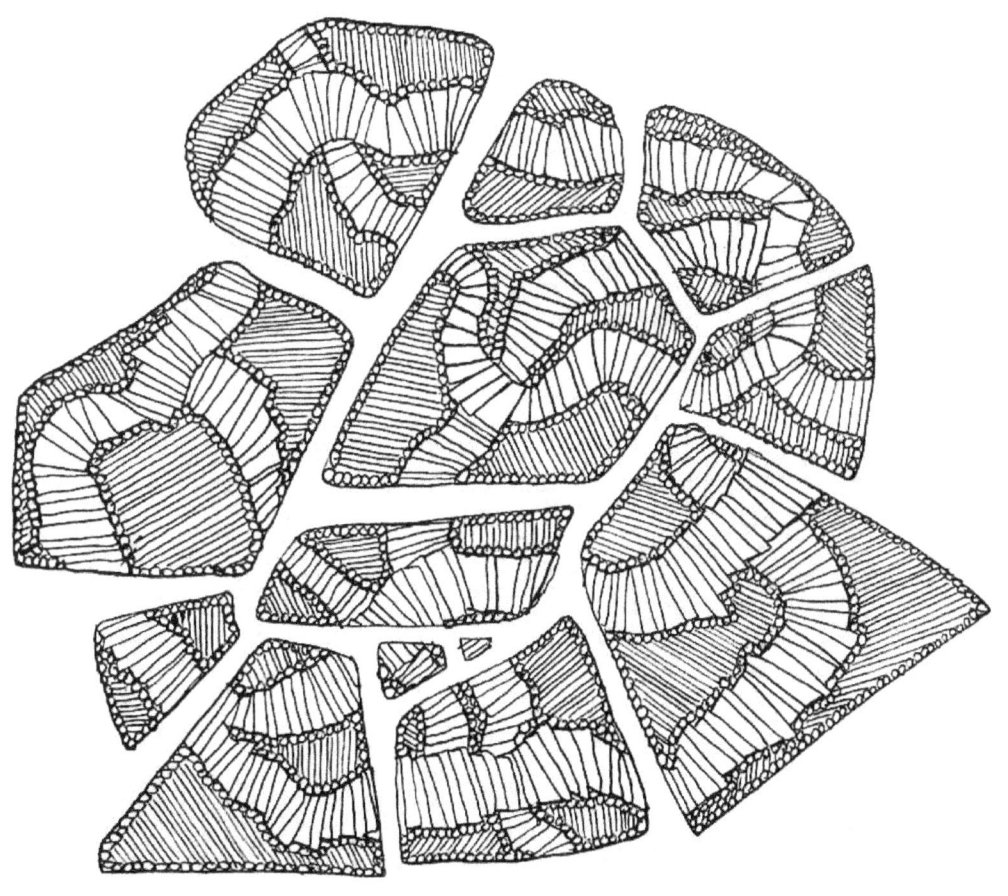

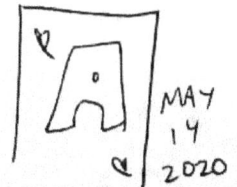

MAY
14
2020

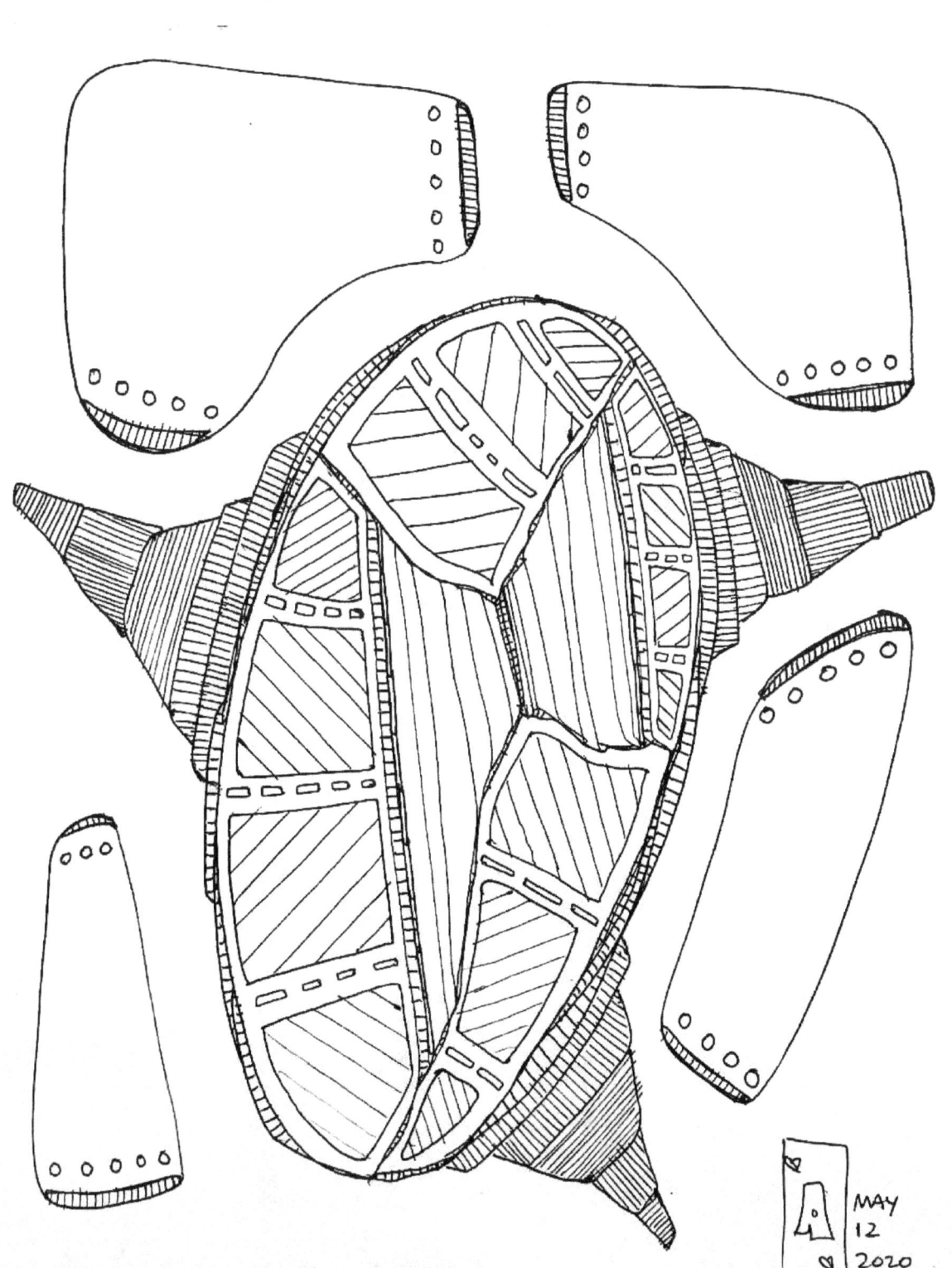

MAY
12
2020

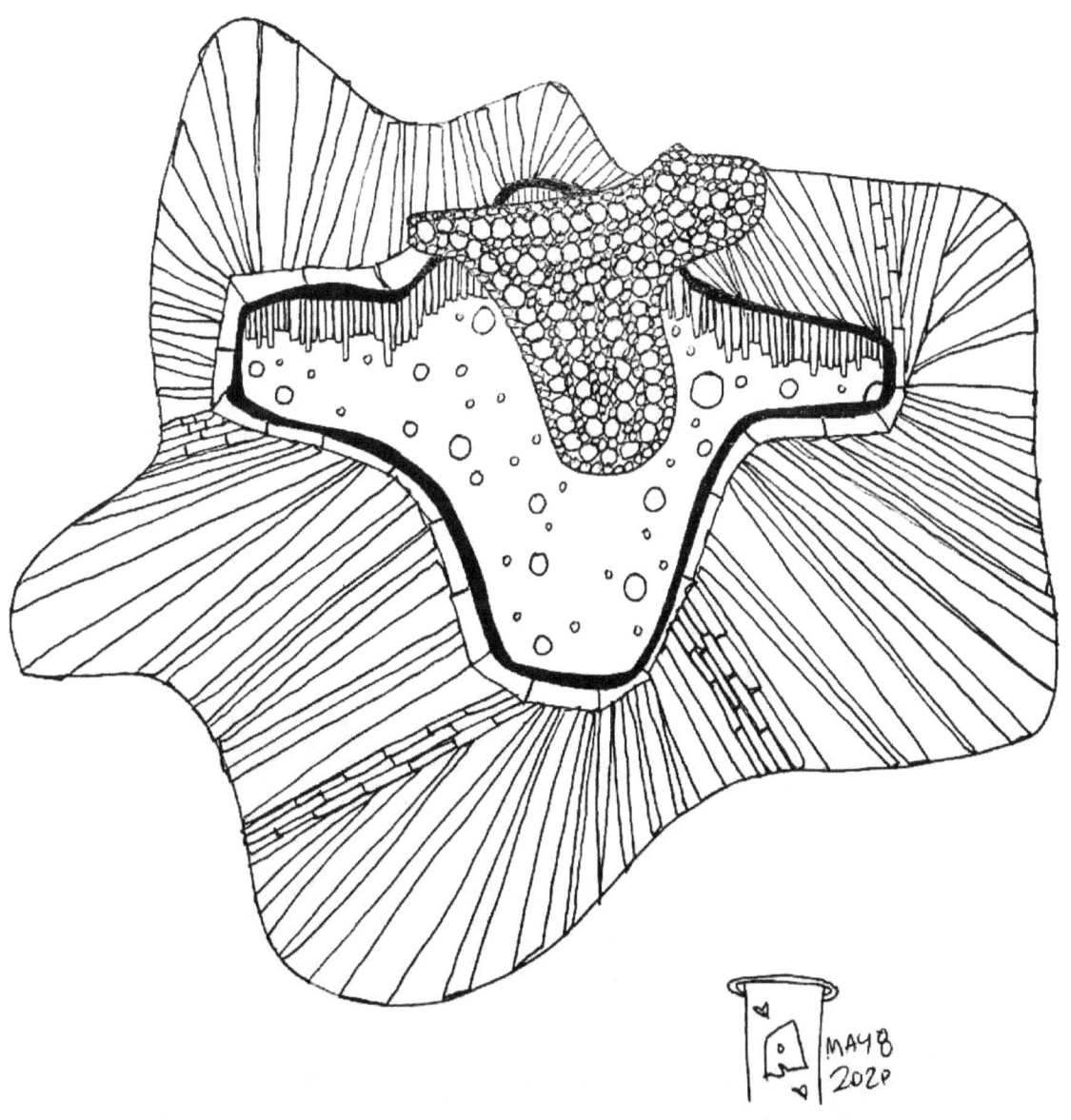

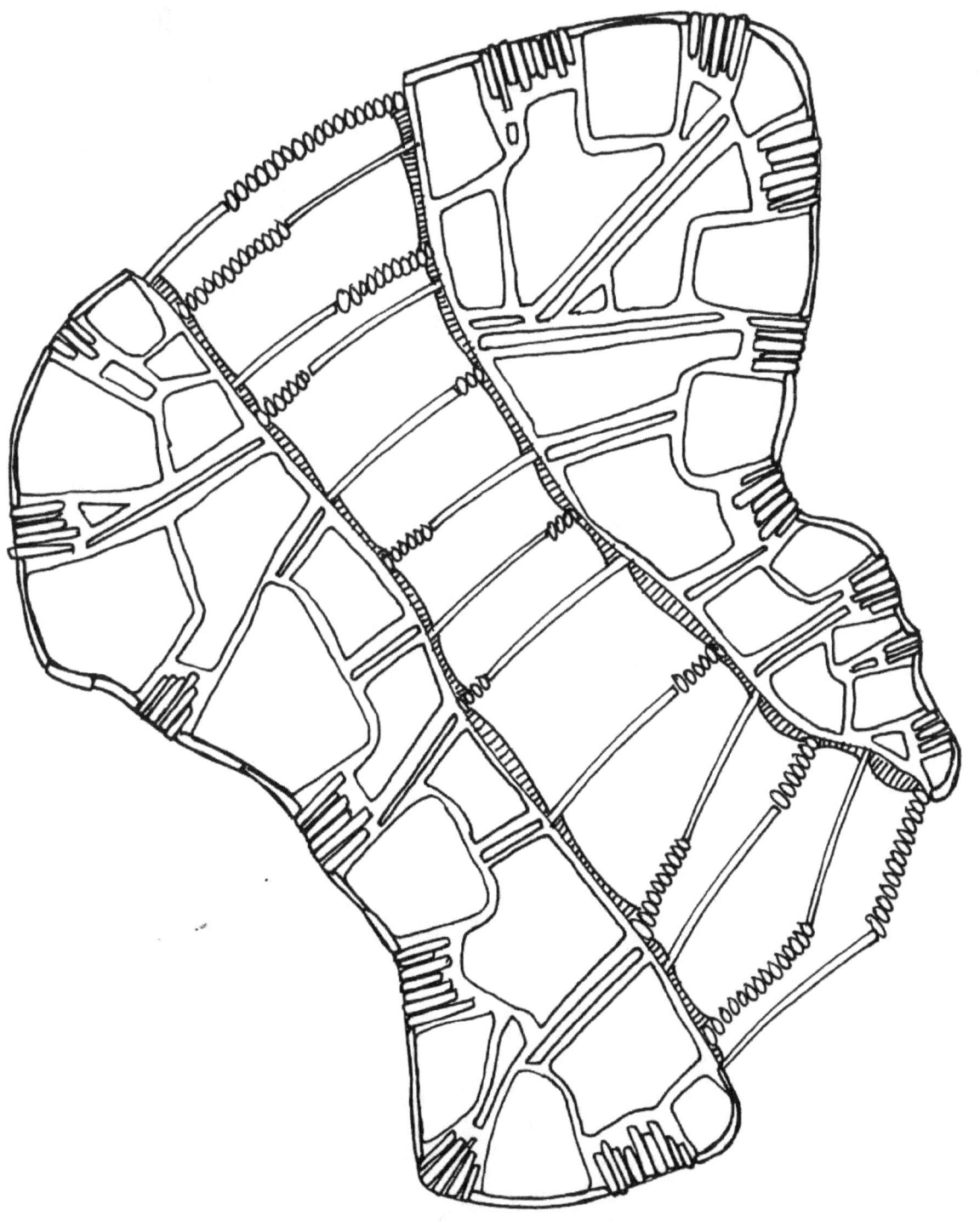

JAN25

NOTE FROM ACE:

THANK YOU FOR CHECKING OUT MY ART! THE ROYALTIES THAT I COLLECT FROM THIS BOOK GO TO HELPING ME CREATE A SUSTAINABLE ECO-FRIENDLY FRUIT FARM IN THE JUNGLE IN HAWAI'I!

FOR MORE INFORMATION ON MY MANY EXCITING PROJECTS CHECK OUT MY INSTAGRAM PROFILE ONLINE: ACE.THEAQUARIAN OR ACE.MAKESART